Spiritual Democracy
and Our Schools

Renewing the American Spirit

with Education for the Whole Child

Steven C. Rockefeller

CLEARVIEW
PUBLISHING

The Collaborative for Spirituality in Education
Teachers College
525 West 120th Street
N.Y., N.Y. 10027

Printed in the United States of America

The new dawn blooms as we free it,
For there is always light,
If only we're brave enough to see it,
If only we're brave enough to be it.

-Amanda Gorman

From *The Hill We Climb,*
An Inaugural Poem for the Country

Contents

Introduction

As the United States enters the third decade of the twenty-first century and approaches the 250th anniversary of the nation's founding, the American people are deeply divided and their democratic republic is seriously troubled. Along with its social, economic, environmental, and political problems, the nation is also contending with critical moral and spiritual challenges. If the nation is to find constructive ways to address the complex crisis it faces, there is an urgent need to awaken a new sense of shared values and common purpose involving a renewed commitment to the animating spirit of American democracy. America's educational system has a vital role to play in this regard. Together with its celebration of freedom, equality, and self-government, the nation has long maintained faith in education as essential to human advancement and the making of engaged, responsible citizens and inspired, strong leaders. This essay is focused on what America's public and independent schools are in a unique position to do at this critical moment in American history.

More specifically, the essay endeavors to support the call coming from a growing number of psychologists, PreK-12 teachers, school administrators, and social activists for education of the whole child – mind, body, heart, and spirit – with special concern for spiritual development, the formation of an intelligent, caring and compassionate way of being. New pathbreaking scientific research supports this transformative educational ideal. Some schools are already successfully showing the way. The well-being of America's young people, revitalization of American democracy, the advance of social justice, protection of Earth's ecological integrity, and safeguarding of the rights of future generations require it.

Early on the essay introduces the concept of spiritual democracy, a relational spirituality that supports widely shared, basic human values as a central theme, providing a way to understand the interconnection of American democracy, spirituality, and education. The meaning of spiritual democracy is clarified as the essay explores the way the insights of philosophers and the research of psychologists and neuroscientists have contributed to a deepening understanding and appreciation of what some psychologists are now calling natural spirituality. The new thinking in this regard views natural spirituality as an innate human capacity that, when nurtured and developed, creates a way of being in relation to self and world that promotes individual freedom and wellbeing, as well as collective flourishing.

Even among those who recognize the need for spirituality in education, there are many public school administrators and teachers who are understandably concerned that public schools cannot talk about and address this sensitive issue without getting entangled in highly contentious debates and legal controversies regarding religion and the schools. The essay will endeavor to explain that even though religion and spirituality are often interrelated, they are not identical, and schools can nurture a young person's inborn spiritual and moral capacities without promoting or opposing religion.

At the outset, it is also important to make clear that there should be no conflict between what schools must do to nurture the spiritual development of young people and maintaining high academic standards. A strong democracy requires citizens proficient in reading, writing, and mathematics and capable of clear, critical thinking. As the essay will point out, there is mounting evidence that creating conditions at school that support the blossoming of a young person's spirit can only help students succeed academically and better prepare them for a productive and rewarding life. The goal is the full integration of academic learning with emotional, social, moral, and spiritual development, recognizing that each young person is a unique individual with special strengths and gifts and that each school will have its distinctive way to advance the goal. Here lies one promising strategy for nurturing in oncoming generations the inner resources and social relationships they must have to lead rewarding lives and serve their communities and country in these turbulent times.

1

The Spiritual Dimension of the Growing Crisis

America finds itself today in a rapidly changing world confronting a host of complex, domestic, and international challenges, from managing the devastating impacts of the coronavirus pandemic to rectifying social and economic injustice, to countering the dangers of climate change and resurgent authoritarianism. It is a time that calls for visionary leadership, cooperative problem solving, political compromise, and unified action. However, the bonds that can bring the American people together in the face of crisis have severely frayed, leaving communities and the nation fractured and fragmented. Even within the nation's two major political parties, there are deep divisions. The government is often rendered dysfunctional by bitter partisan politics and well-financed special interests. Pressing social, economic, and environmental problems go unaddressed with potentially catastrophic, long-term consequences for people and the planet. The most shocking and shameful example of government dysfunction is the nation's failure to protect children and teachers from being attacked and killed in schools by deranged young men armed with military-style assault weapons. After decades of inaction, following the most recent school massacre in Uvalde, Texas, the United States Congress was finally able to marshal the bipartisan support needed to take some modest steps to address gun violence. However, there is so much more that can and should be done.

The causes of this state of the nation are many, including a culture of self-centered individualism, rising inequality in wealth and income, stagnation in social mobility, a reckoning over racial discrimination, the deep resentments and struggle for power associated with identity politics, and a hate-filled ideological battle between the nation's two major political parties fueled to a large extent by culture wars, social media, and extremism on the Right and the Left. Political opponents are demonized and a willingness to compromise is viewed as a betrayal. In *The Upswing: How America Came Together a Century Ago and We Can Do It Again* (2020), Robert Putnam, Professor of Public Policy at Harvard University, convincingly argues that what the nation is experiencing today is the consequence of over five decades of intensifying self-centeredness, tribalism, and declining national solidarity that began in the late 1960s: "The majority of Americans are in the grip of an ethos and mindset focused on me, not we," asserts Putnam.[1]

Under the impact of polarization, pandemic, and economic hardship, the mood of the country tends to be anxious, angry, and pessimistic. Large numbers of people feel unrecognized, excluded, and alienated. Trust in the nation's major institutions and the elite that manage them has plummeted. The meaning of American history, the narrative we tell ourselves about who we are as a people, and how it should be taught, is being contested in communities across the country, undermining a sense of shared national identity, and shaking many citizens' belief in America. There has also been a steep decline in respect for reason, science, and truth as well as a decline in religious faith and participation in organized religion. Crime and violence are growing problems. Many citizens turn to fantastic conspiracy theories to make sense of what they view as a hostile, chaotic world. Groups on the Left and the Right endeavor to curtail freedom of speech in ways that obstruct the kind of honest, open sharing of experience and search for truth and understanding that is fundamental to the workings of democracy. Some activists and educators have forgotten that one cannot build a free and democratic society with authoritarian tactics. The January 6, 2021 assault on the nation's capital by a violent mob intent on overturning the results of a presidential election makes clear that democracy itself has come under attack. Fear, anxiety, cynicism, depression, and despair are widespread. Deaths of despair by drug overdose, alcohol poisoning, and suicide have reached alarming levels among young people as well as adults. The Office of the Surgeon General, the American Academy of Pediatrics, and the Centers for Disease Control and Prevention have all declared a national crisis and emergency in child and adolescent mental health.

Any serious endeavor to overcome this multi-dimensional crisis gripping the nation will have to find ways to address the deeper source of the condition in which the American people find themselves. The underlying problem is the erosion and weakening of America's moral and spiritual foundations, reflecting estrangement from our better selves and one another and the larger community of life on Earth. So many of the country's leaders and ordinary citizens have lost faith in a shared set of core American values that are considered sacred, transcend all political and social differences, and provide a unifying sense of national identity and common purpose. As a number of leaders have asserted, America is a nation in search of its soul. There is an urgent need for a rediscovery of ideals and values that can once again serve as an inspiring, healing, and unifying force.

In 2018, the American Academy of Arts and Sciences created a bipartisan Commission on The Practice of Democratic Citizenship and charged the Commission to explore ways to address the worsening crisis. Two years later the Commission issued its report to the nation, "Our Common Purpose: Reinventing American Democracy for the 21st Century." The Report includes an urgent call for the renewal of "the spiritual, moral, and intellectual foundations of democracy." Its recommendations emphasize two broad interrelated strategies. The first involves implementing a long list of reforms in the way the country's major institutions operate to make them more resilient and effective. The second is "the imperative...to inspire a culture of commitment to America's constitutional democracy and one another." The report explains that the goal of this national "culture of commitment" should be nothing less than the formation of ethically responsible citizens guided by the "democratic faith" and "love of country and one another." The report also recognizes that schools have an important role to play in renewing American democracy, and it emphasizes the need for expanding and improving civic education.[2]

In addition to "love of country and one another," there is also need for a national culture in the twenty-first century that cultivates in the American people a love of nature and planet Earth, our home in the universe. Humanity is an interdependent member of the greater community of life, and human development and thriving are dependent on preserving the health of Earth's ecological systems. Ongoing ecological degradation by industrial-technological societies, including global warming and destruction of the planet's biodiversity, if not reversed, puts the future survival of the human species at risk. Respect and care for the greater community of life and sustainable development have become essential aspects of ethically responsible democratic citizenship. Since we live in an increasingly interdependent world in which the local and the global are interconnected ecologically, economically, and socially, responsible citizenship includes a sense of global citizenship. In the words of the Earth Charter, an international declaration of principles for building a just, sustainable, and peaceful world launched in 2000, "We are one human family and one Earth Community with a common destiny."[3] We will return to these issues in later sections of the essay.

One ray of light in the midst of these troubled times is that most Americans still thrill at the singing of the national anthem and want to believe that America has a higher moral purpose, and across the country, there is a growing yearning for major change. Robert Gipe, an Appalachian writer and educator, gave expression to what many Americans are feeling and thinking in the following statement:

We all crave honorable work at a living wage. We want success tied to the success of the community. We want to be safe. We are weary of fear. We are exhausted by hate. We in Appalachia join our fellow Americans in asking: Who will encourage our best selves? Who will enable our joy? Who will release the energy hiding in our hearts?[4]

These three concluding questions are prophetic, especially the call to awaken "the energy hiding in our hearts." They give expression to the most fundamental challenge facing America. The knowledge generated by rational analysis and the sciences is critical to building a better world but not sufficient. It can explain the causal connections between things and the nature of problems and provides the ability to control the world in significant ways. It can clarify critical moral and spiritual problems and elucidate the consequences of different choices. However, by itself, it cannot compel action. It remains up to human beings in their freedom to decide what kind of a person they want to be and what quality of human relationships and community life they want to create and sustain. In this regard, unless the knowledge generated by the sciences is integrated with the wisdom and caring generated by an open heart, it is not sufficient to guide the change needed. "If you really want to open your mind, open your heart first," advises the moral psychologist, Jonathan Haidt.[5]

In *Healing the Heart of Democracy* (2011), Parker Palmer, the educator and activist, defines the "heart" as our deep inner core in a manner consistent with much spiritual literature.

"Heart" comes from the Latin *cor* and points not merely to our emotions but to the core of the self, that center place where all our ways of knowing converge – intellectual, emotional, sensory, intuitive, imaginative, experiential, relational, and bodily, among others. The heart is where we integrate what we know in our minds with what we know in our bones, the place where our knowledge can become more fully human…It is where we can learn to "think the world together," not apart, and find the courage to act on what we know…For those of us who want to see democracy thrive – and we are legion – the heart is where everything begins: that grounded place in each of us where we can overcome fear, rediscover that we are members of one another, and embrace the conflicts that threaten democracy as openings to new life for us and for our nation.[6]

The "energy hiding in our hearts" is a transformative spiritual force that is blocked when our hearts are closed and hardened and is released when our hearts are freed from the illusion of separateness and opened. The essence of this liberating spiritual energy is caring, compassion, and love, which inspires our best selves, and when joined with intelligence it can heal and create rewarding relationships and build inclusive, just communities. Here lies the wellspring of the true spirit of American democracy. It is those who embrace this spirit who "will enable our joy."

Some critics, who view democratic politics as just a brutal struggle for power among tribal factions, may dismiss the call for a transformative, national, ethical culture as impractical sentimental idealism. Such cynicism regarding human nature and democracy is part of the problem. The spirit of caring, compassion, and love is the deeper source of the democratic ideal and way of life. It is this spirit that inspires recognition and respect for the freedom, equal dignity, and equal rights of every person and calls for commitment to the rule of law, justice for all, and the common good. Before focusing directly on the role of education and schools, it is important to further clarify this understanding of the relational spirituality that supports American democracy.

2

Democracy as an Ethical Ideal and Way of Life

In general, people tend to think of democracy as a political system, a form of government. However, it is more than that. American democracy is best understood as first and foremost a great ethical ideal and way of life. Alexis de Tocqueville came to this realization when he traveled across the country in the 1830s in search of an understanding of the dynamics of the new nation's democracy. He presented his findings in *Democracy in America*, emphasizing "the habits of the heart" that guided American citizens as they built a vibrant civil society and engaged in the processes of self-government. A relational spirituality that nurtures a deep faith in ethical values and shapes a person's way of being in all their relationships, what this essay will call spiritual democracy, is the foundation of political democracy. Coming to this understanding as a graduate student in the 1960s at Columbia University after reading John Dewey, America's leading philosopher and educational reformer during the early decades of the twentieth century, was for me a real awakening. Viewing democracy as a great ethical ideal and way of life as well as a political system opened a way to integrate spiritual life and secular life in modern society and to transform both. In developing a further understanding of this idea, it is useful to begin with the thinking of the nation's founders, who, despite whatever moral deficiencies they exhibited as individuals, did something truly exceptional and of world-historical significance in founding the United States of America. It will also be instructive to consider Dewey's vision and other related thinkers.

The founders of the American democratic republic contended that their experiment in creating a free, self-governing society could only succeed if it had a moral and spiritual foundation. Their commitment to individual freedom and autonomy as a core democratic ideal reflects a certain basic faith in human nature – in the human capacity for reason, moral responsibility, cooperation, kindness, and justice. However, they were also well aware of the Christian doctrine of sin and the warnings in classical philosophy regarding the dangers created by ignorance and the passions. They understood the strong influence of self-interest in human nature and knew that power corrupts. Given their view of human nature, they firmly believed that freedom without wisdom and virtue – without self-knowledge, self-discipline, and a high sense of moral and social responsibility is unsustainable. In their judgment, if the American people were to be united and to build together a just and prosperous society, the new nation required highly educated leaders with exceptional intelligence and moral integrity and an educated citizenry with an awakened conscience.

A constitution with multiple checks and balances was designed that prevents the centralization of power in the hands of any one person, guards against the abuse of power, and provides for the impeachment of presidents who become demagogues and a threat to the republic. It was widely thought at the time that even though human beings have a natural capacity for empathy, sympathy, and benevolence, these moral and altruistic feelings so important to sustaining community have to be carefully supported and nurtured. In this regard, they looked to the family, religion, and schools as having critical roles to play. In his Farewell Address to the People of the United States after serving two terms as the nation's first president, George Washington, declared "wisdom and virtue" to be "the great pillars of human happiness" and "the foundation of…free government." Any free society that ignores the insights and understanding of the founders in these matters does so at its peril.[7]

In the midst of significant cultural and religious diversity, what brought a majority of the American colonists together in support of the revolution for independence and the founding of the nation was faith in shared moral and political ideals. The transformative vision at the heart of this faith is set forth prominently early in the Declaration of Independence.

> We hold these truths to be self-evident, that all men are created equal, that they are endowed by their Creator with certain unalienable Rights, that among these are Life, Liberty, and the pursuit of Happiness. – That to secure these rights, Governments are instituted among Men, deriving their just powers from the consent of the governed.

The issuing of the Declaration of Independence with its radical affirmation of the principles of equality, freedom, and unalienable rights marks the beginning of the founding of the nation. The Constitution does not reaffirm the Declaration's principle of equality. However, when defining the nation's fundamental ideals and values, leaders like Abraham Lincoln have persuasively argued that the Declaration of Independence should have priority over the Constitution and the Constitution should be read with the understanding that the Declaration's affirmation of human equality is its guiding spirit.[8] This position was strongly supported by the anti-slavery movement leading up to and during the Civil War and has been widely accepted by all who support a vision of inclusive community and battle racism, bigotry, intolerance, and injustice in whatever form it takes.

The ideals and values that form the core of the American creed are further elaborated in the Preamble of the Constitution, which was ratified by the thirteen states in 1791.

> We the People of the United States, in Order to form a more perfect Union, establish Justice, insure domestic Tranquility, provide for the common defense, promote the general Wel-

fare, and secure the Blessings of Liberty to ourselves and our Posterity, do ordain and establish this Constitution for the United States of America.

The Constitution makes clear that America is to be a nation governed by the sovereignty of "the people" and the rule of law, not the arbitrary will of a king or other tyrant. The Preamble highlights the values of liberty, unity, justice, peace, national security, the common good, and intergenerational responsibility. Early on the nation adopted the motto, *E Pluribus Unum*, out of many one, emphasizing the vital importance of shared values, a common identity, and national solidarity in a nation of diverse peoples that also celebrates the ideal of individual autonomy.

Regarding the overarching purpose of the new American republic, James Madison, the chief drafter of the Constitution, declared that "the public good, the real welfare of the great body of the people, is the supreme object to be pursued."[9] The founders considered the essence of responsible political leadership and civic virtue to be devotion to the common good and a readiness to sacrifice self-interest for the public interest. In addition, the founders imagined American citizens being united by the spirit of mutual affection, goodwill, cooperation, and benevolence. In short, as the ideal of striving for "a more perfect Union" and the motto *E Pluribus Unum* suggest, the creation of America as a democratic republic was understood to be a great spiritual and moral undertaking as well as a pathbreaking political experiment.

It is also the case that major aspects of the social and economic structure of eighteenth-century American society stood in contradiction to the ideals of freedom and equality set forth in the Declaration of Independence. These contradictions are reflected in the lives of the founders and influenced the drafting of the Constitution, and they would remain forces shaping American history with tragic, long-term consequences. Colonial America was a patriarchal society and women were not considered to be equal to men. The new Constitution did not grant women the right to vote, and it would be over a century before women secured this basic right of an American citizen. The Constitution did not recognize the rights of Native Americans, and they were driven from their lands and suffered the destruction of their cultures and way of life. There were over 700,000 enslaved persons in the United States at the time the Constitution was ratified in 1791. The greatest flaw in the Constitution is that in a compromise designed to keep the Southern states in the Union, it allowed perpetuation of the evil of slavery in those states that did not outlaw it and continuation of the slave trade until 1807. The New England states did outlaw slavery. A number of the founders were slaveholders, including Thomas Jefferson and George Washington. Most viewed slavery as morally abhorrent and feared the consequences of its perpetuation. Washington freed his slaves in his will, and President Jefferson signed into law legislation banning the slave trade in 1808. Explaining why the founders were led to permit a great evil to become part of the new nation, James Madison wrote: "Great as the evil is, a dismemberment of the Union would be worse."[10] It would require a devastating civil war that took the lives of over 600,000 men and the adoption of the Thirteenth, Fourteenth, and Fifteenth Amendments to end slavery and grant African-American men the right to vote. In the twenty-first century, the nation finds itself still struggling with the legacy of slavery and the persistence of racism.

The story of the founding and the nation's history since then raises disturbing moral issues and that moral complexity is being examined and debated today by historians as never before. However, contemporary reconstructions of American history will not alter a basic, long-standing principle regarding what defines an American citizen as an American. It is not a matter of religion, race, or ethnic origin even though some have tried to make such claims. It is a shared faith in the ethical and political ideals proclaimed in the Declaration of Independence and the Constitution with its amendments that defines an American as an American and forms our national identity. These ideals and values are the heart of the beliefs and rituals that some social scientists and philosophers have labeled America's civil religion. One can deplore the history of racial injustice, the brutal oppression of Native Americans, the inequality of women, and other ways the reality of American society has contradicted the nation's ideals, and at the same time embrace the American democratic faith and experiment in democracy.

Langston Hughes, the Harlem Renaissance poet and activist makes this point and speaks for all marginalized and oppressed groups when in the 1930s during the Depression he wrote:

Let America be America again.

Let it be the dream it used to be…

The land that never has been yet-

And yet must be…

America never was America to me,

And yet I swear this oath-

America will be![11]

As the Civil Rights Movement was gaining momentum in the early 1960s, James Baldwin in *The Fire Next Time* raged against the brutality of racism and social injustice in America and warned that without real change the nation faced an explosive situation. He also retained Langston Hughes' faith in America's core ideals and in the possibility that people, whatever their skin color, can change for the better. In a public letter to his nephew, he encouraged him and other young Black Americans to join the struggle, declaring "we can make America what America must become." Baldwin recognized the need for power to effect change, but he also argues that love, not hate, is the only sure guide to a way forward.[12]

Martin Luther King, Jr., the leader of the civil rights movement, understood the foundation of American democracy to be moral or spiritual democracy, and in his speeches, like Langston Hughes, he called upon America to embrace the original American dream involving freedom, equality, and national solidarity. He believed that the deeper meaning of American democracy is found in the realization "that God made us to live together as brothers and sisters and to respect the dignity and worth" of every person. The ideal and goal is nothing less than the "creation of the beloved community" in the midst of the nation's great diversity. King was a Christian realist regarding the forces of sin and evil in the world, but he also believed that love is a powerful, creative force and that "the arc of the moral universe is long but it tends towards justice."[13]

The nation's founding ideals, the original American dream, articulate universal human aspirations and the promise of American democracy. However, we live in a world where the struggle against evil is real. It goes on within the heart of every individual, within every society, in every generation. Given the prevalence of ignorance, the influence of narrow self-interest, and the corruption generated by money and power, advancing freedom, equality, and justice is a never-ending task that each generation must take up anew and redefine for its time. American society has undergone massive change over its 250-year history, and it remains an ongoing work in progress. Self-criticism is built into the American democratic system, and the democratic faith and the aspirations it evokes are the fundamental force driving social change and the advance of human rights, social justice, and the common good. In her stirring poem presented at President Joe Biden's 2021 inauguration, Amanda Gorman asserts that America "isn't broken, but simply unfinished," and she concludes:

The new dawn blooms as we free it,

For there is always light,

If only we're brave enough to see it,

If only we're brave enough to be it.[14]

Our way of being as Americans and what we want America to become, is the deeper, critical issue and the concern of spiritual democracy.

The concept of moral or spiritual democracy is most fully developed in John Dewey's early and later thought. Under the influence of the nineteenth century Neo-Hegelian philosophical tradition and inspired by Walt Whitman's vision in "Democratic Vistas," early in his career in an essay on the "Ethics of Democracy," Dewey declared that "Democracy and the one, ultimate ethical ideal of humanity are synonyms" and that political democracy is an outgrowth of commitment to this universal ethical ideal. The ethics of democracy, he argued, should govern all human relations, in the home, school, and workplace as well as in the political sphere. These convictions led him to envision the emergence in America of a democratic society in which spiritual life and everyday life are integrated and "the distinction between the spiritual and the secular has ceased."[15]

In addition, even though Dewey, as a young Neo-Hegelian philosopher in the 1880s, closely associated the supreme ethical ideal and moral democracy with basic Christian ethical ideals, he came to believe that the development of the spiritual and ethical life so fundamental to a vibrant democracy is not necessarily dependent on organized religion. His daughter explains that Dewey's wife, Alice Chipman, "had a deeply religious nature but had never accepted any religious dogma," and he "acquired from her the belief that a religious attitude is indigenous to natural experience" and can develop independently and apart from institutional religion. By emphasizing that a relational spirituality "indigenous to natural experience" lies at the heart of the democratic way of life, opening the way to an integration of spiritual life and everyday life in the modern world, Dewey was endeavoring to create an alternative to institutional forms of religion that for many modern women and men had become devoid of vital meaning and also to inspire the transformation of those social and economic structures in the secular world that are dehumanizing and unjust.[16]

Young Dewey's optimism regarding social change was tempered by twentieth-century politics and world war, but he never lost his democratic faith and hope. Toward the end of his career in the 1930s, long after he had developed his own distinctive brand of philosophical naturalism and humanism, he reaffirmed and further clarified his belief in the deeper meaning of democracy. In *Freedom and Culture* (1939), he writes:

> ...the source of the American democratic tradition is moral – not technical, abstract, narrowly political nor materially utilitarian. It is moral because based on faith in the ability of human nature to achieve freedom for individuals accompanied with respect and regard for other persons and with social stability built on cohesion instead of coercion.[17]

That same year at a celebration of his 80th birthday in a talk entitled "Creative Democracy – The Task Before Us," he declares that "Democracy is a moral ideal, and so far as it is a fact, it is a moral fact." More specifically, he defines democracy as "a personal way of individual life" that involves "possession and continued use of certain attitudes, forming personal character and determining desire and purpose in all the relations of life."[18] In this regard, he often refers to moral democracy and social democracy. He did not use the term spiritual democracy in his later thought. However, in *A Common Faith* (1934), he argues that "the religious dimension of experience" can be developed apart from institutional religion, and he explains that wholehearted commitment to the democratic faith and way of life can generate a sustaining sense of meaning and purpose and have a unifying effect on a person's life and relation with the world that is deeply religious (spiritual) in quality. He called for creating communities and schools with a democratic culture and ethos that promotes "personal growth in mind and spirit" and plants the seeds of, and cultivates, just such a faith. Regarding the role of the schools, Dewey commented that "democracy has to be born anew every generation, and education is its midwife."[19]

Dewey's vision of the democratic way of life puts a special emphasis on the intellectual, moral, and spiritual growth of the individual and on "free and open communication" leading to "shared experience" and the building of community. "The democratic way of life commits us," writes Dewey, "to increasing effort to break down the walls of class, of unequal opportunity, of color, race, sect, and nationality, which estrange human beings from one another." His life experience led him to celebrate shared experience as the most effective way to overcome the bigotry, intolerance, and oppression that divide and fragment society. Among the democratic attitudes and virtues highlighted in his essays are: "faith in the potentialities of human nature" when education and the right conditions for human development are provided; faith in the collaborative scientific search for truth and the future of the social sciences as sources of practical guidance; "intelligent sympathy" – opening one's mind and heart to the interests, suffering, and rights of others; and the spirit of cooperation, nonviolence, and peace. Dewey's call for "intelligent sympathy" in the democratic way of life was the language he used to stress the vital importance of empathy and compassion coupled with the understanding generated by reason and science. Dewey also cautioned that since the means used determine the ends achieved, a society cannot advance democratic ends with undemocratic means.[20]

In an essay on "Search for the Great Community," he asserts that "democracy is a name for a life of free and enriching communion." Regarding the rewards and joy that the democratic life promises, he writes: "When the emotional force, the mystic force one might say, of communication, of the miracle of shared life and shared experience is spontaneously felt, the hardness and crudeness of contemporary life will be bathed in the light that never was on land or sea." Dewey's democratic faith and communitarianism involve a relational spirituality and ethical mysticism that the historian of philosophy, John Herman Randall Jr., describes as his "religion of shared experience."[21]

Dewey's overarching objective as a philosopher is to explore ways to overcome the separation of the ideal and the real in twentieth-century industrial-technological society, and his philosophy regarding natural spirituality and democracy as a great moral ideal and way of life is a central part of his larger vision. As a philosophical naturalist, he believed that there is one world, the world of nature, and he abandoned the idea of the supernatural. Further, long before the emergence of the science of ecology, Dewey formed a deep appreciation of the interdependence of humanity and nature. His outlook in this regard involves an attitude of piety toward nature and a sustaining personal sense of belonging to the universe and cosmic trust supported by emotional intuitions of a mystical nature. In addition, he wisely advised that respect and care for the larger natural world should be an essential aspect of the spiritual life of a modern democratic society seeking to realize the ideal possibilities of life on Earth.[22]

3 | Spiritual Democracy for the Twenty-First Century

There are six interrelated principles that form the moral and spiritual ideal at the center of the American democratic faith and the original American dream: freedom, equality, human rights, the rule of law, justice, and the common good. These ideals have deep roots in over three thousand years of Western spiritual, intellectual, moral, social, and political evolution. Spiritual democracy encompasses all the values and virtues that have inspired the formulation of these great ideals and that are required to advance and implement them. The interrelationship and tension

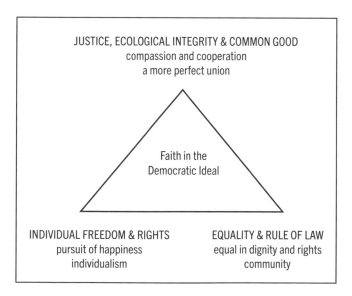

Fig. 1, The Spiritual and Moral Ideal at the heart of American Democracy

between these six principles are suggested in Figure 1. From the perspective of the twenty-first century, the democratic faith should include one additional fundamental principle: Respect and care for the greater community of life, which involves adopting sustainable ways of living and safeguarding Earth's ecological integrity – its biological diversity, regenerative capacities, and natural beauty.

Freedom and equality are the two most radical ideals promoted by the American Revolution. Freedom is the most cherished American ideal and is celebrated in the statues of Liberty atop the nation's capital and on Liberty Island in New York Harbor as well as in songs, sermons, and political movements. However, the way freedom is understood and defined makes all the difference. Philosophers distinguish between negative freedom, freedom from oppression and restraint, and positive freedom, what people use their freedom for and what ideals and values they choose to support and serve. The development and exercise of positive freedom determine what kind of persons we become, our way of being, and the quality of the relationships and community life we sustain. It is important to keep in mind that restraint may be inner as well as external. Ignorance, fear, hatred, desire, and hopelessness can bind and restrain as well as oppressive external forces. A person in the grip of delusion and blind passions is not free. For this reason, the world's great spiritual traditions put special emphasis on inner liberation as the necessary foundation for social liberation. In this regard, it is noteworthy that in the Socratic tradition, which the founders knew well, "the pursuit of happiness" had a profound meaning. The classical Greek concept of happiness (*eudaimonia*) involves a holistic view of wellbeing that includes the full realization of a person's intellectual, aesthetic, moral, and spiritual capacities.

Among those Americans fighting for independence in the Revolution, freedom meant at a minimum the right to pursue their individual dreams and happiness guided by their own experience and intelligence without interference from the government. However, if individual freedom is identified primarily with the absence of external restraint and is reduced to a self-centered, atomistic individualism, which has been an all-too-common phenomenon at different periods in American history, including the present, it can undermine efforts to promote equality, social justice, and the common good. Tribalism takes hold. The bonds of community fray. Wealth and power are concentrated in the hands of the few. The strong exploit the weak. The natural environment is degraded. Democracy is corrupted. Alienation, mistrust, resentment, anger, hatred, depression, and spiritual emptiness spread.

The principle of equality challenges a narrow, self-centered understanding of freedom and the pursuit of happiness. It mandates that with freedom and the rights of citizenship goes ethical responsibilities in relation to others. It calls for building strong, inclusive, cohesive institutions and communities that support human rights, opportunity and justice for all, and the promotion of the common good. The basic meaning of the principle of equality is stated concisely in Article 1 of the Universal Declaration of Human Rights adopted by the United Nations in 1948: "All human beings are born free and equal in dignity and rights." The Declaration of Independence proclaimed that "all men are created equal" and most Americans at the time understood men to mean white men. The explicit reference to "all human beings" in the UN Declaration, which was drafted by an international commission chaired by Eleanor Roosevelt, reflects the ongoing struggle in America and globally to overcome the painful and tragic history of sexism, racism, intolerance, oppression, and discrimination in all its forms.

The original inspiration leading, over many centuries, to the development of the ideal of equality in America is found in biblical religion and the idea that human beings are created in the image of God and possess immeasurable intrinsic value. This ancient worldview suggests that there is something sacred about every person and the development of their unique potential. This outlook inspired the prophetic call in the Bible to treat others with kindness and to establish justice. The Bible's Golden Rule, which is affirmed in all the world's great religious traditions, articulates the general ethical guideline: "In everything do to others as you would have them do to you; for this is the law and the prophets." (Matthew 7:12) This universal ethical principle invites us, amid all our differences, to identify with the other as a person with whom we share a common humanity and who like us seeks to find happiness and to avoid harm and suffering. It encourages an attitude of empathy and compassion. It involves relating to others first and foremost, not as representatives of various groups with which one may or not identify, but as fellow human beings endowed with dignity and worthy of respect and care. It is vitally important to appreciate the many ways people and cultures are different, but when the overwhelming emphasis is on our different identities, as is often the case in contemporary America, it promotes separatism and leaves people without a sense of what on a very basic level they have in common and that can sustain community in the midst of diversity. In this regard, it is noteworthy that when President Lincoln in his Second Inaugural Address endeavored to inspire the American people following the Civil War to find a path to recovery, reconciliation, and "a just and lasting peace among ourselves," he invoked the spirit of the Golden Rule. In his concluding words, he summoned the nation to come together to undertake this daunting task "with malice toward none, with charity for all."

In the Universal Declaration of Human Rights, the theological language used in the Bible and by Thomas Jefferson in the Declaration of Independence and by Lincoln is gone but the spirit of the ancient ideal remains. The declaration that all human beings are "equal in dignity" is an affirmation of their intrinsic value and our common humanity, and it supports the moral imperative that one should always treat other persons as an end and never as a means only.[23] Human rights endeavor to identify the conditions that are essential for human development and that are fundamental to the common good and building a society that honors human dignity. The idea that all human beings are "equal in dignity and rights" is consistent with the moral guideline in the Golden Rule, the call to treat others with the same respect, understanding, and compassion with which one would like to be treated. It supports the call to recognize the ignored, protect the vulnerable, and build civil dialogue and cooperative working relationships that can hold together a pluralistic, democratic society. So many of the problems facing America today, including economic inequality, racism, anti-Semitism, sexual assault, discrimination based on sexual orientation, and hate-filled, partisan politics, are rooted in a failure to respect and honor the inherent dignity and equal rights of the other.[24] Moreover, this failure reveals a great weakness in the nation's educational systems.

A healthy democratic society requires strong institutions in all spheres – family life, civil society, business, and government. People are dependent upon and sustained by these institutions, and they have a moral responsibility to serve and sustain them. There is a tendency among educated people in Western industrialized consumer societies to think of the self as a discreet, autonomous entity existing apart from its relationships and to focus primarily on the rights of the individual, failing to appreciate the interdependence of the self and the community, the needs of institutions, and the duties of the individual in relation to these institutions. A healthy, strong democratic society must find intelligent ways to balance the needs of individuals and the needs of institutions, the rights of citizens and the duties of citizens. It must promote reforms that address the demand for social and economic justice but also endeavor to avoid rapid changes with unintended, harmful, social consequences. In this regard, America can benefit from the moral concerns and insights of both conservatives and liberals as it endeavors to chart the way forward with regard to these issues.[25]

When exploring the meaning of spiritual democracy in the twenty-first century, it is essential to include consideration of humanity's relationship with nature, the ecological responsibilities of citizens, and the importance of a sense of global citizenship. With industrialization, technological innovation, and economic globalization, an interconnected, multicultural, global civilization is being constructed, greatly increasing the interdependence of all peoples and the need for international cooperation. In addition, over the past fifty years, the Earth sciences have revealed that our planet's biosphere is one great, interrelated ecological system, of which humanity is an interdependent part, and human patterns of production and consumption and human population growth are severely stressing this complex system. These developments are generating a new holistic, planetary consciousness that includes an ethical and spiritual dimension, which finds expression in, for example, the development of international human rights law, initiatives to end poverty worldwide, and visionary documents like the World Charter for Nature (1982), the Earth Charter (2000), and the UN Sustainable Development Goals (2015). Spiritual democracy in the twenty-first century involves taking the emerging international vision of universal ethical values to heart and supporting the United Nations and its efforts to build a just, sustainable, and peaceful world. The negative impact of some forms of economic globalization has generated protests and a surge in nationalism in many countries. Nations do have a first responsibility to address local needs, but in an interdependent world, the local and the global cannot be neatly separated, especially concerning environmental issues. In accordance with their different capacities, all peoples are called to be responsible global citizens.

In the twenty-first century, protecting and restoring Earth's ecological integrity and living sustainably within the carrying capacity of the planet's ecological system has become an essential aspect of any sound democratic vision of social justice and the common good. First, it is a matter of human self-interest and basic ethical responsibilities mandated by the Constitution. The degradation of the environment, including global warming and the destruction of Earth's biodiversity and beauty, is disrupting the livelihoods and undermining the health – physical, emotional, and spiritual – of millions of people worldwide, especially the disadvantaged and poor. In addition, the Constitution recognizes the vital importance of intergenerational responsibility when it asserts that American citizens and their government are duty bound to "secure the Blessings of Liberty for ourselves and our Posterity." Future generations have a right to a clean, healthy, and beautiful natural environment, and ongoing environmental degradation not only denies them this right, but also has the potential to undermine their efforts to realize the core democratic ideal of an "unalienable Right" to "Life, Liberty, and the pursuit of Happiness."

Second, if the environmentally destructive patterns of consumption and production in modern societies are to be radically and rapidly changed, it will require more than a heightened sense of intergenerational responsibility. What is also needed is an expansion of humanity's sense of community and ethical consciousness to include a compassionate concern for the wellbeing of the other life forms with whom human beings share planet Earth. Fundamental to the new ecological consciousness is the spiritual and scientifically informed realization that human beings are interdependent members of the greater community of life on Earth, and as citizens of the Earth community, people have responsibilities in relation to the other members of the community and the community as a whole.

The emerging ecological consciousness recognizes that the dominant attitude toward the larger natural world in industrial-technological societies is misguided. This problematical outlook reflects a dualism, a separation, of human culture and the larger world of nature that reduces nature to a collection of resources that has utilitarian value only and exists for the sole purpose of human exploitation. Contemporary environmental ethics rejects this anthropocentric attitude, which is a fundamental cause of environmental devastation, and asserts that all life forms have intrinsic value quite apart from their utilitarian value for people and are worthy of humanity's respect, love, and care. As Thomas Berry, the cultural historian and environmental philosopher, has contended: "The universe is a communion of subjects, not a collection of objects."[26] In this regard, a growing number of environmentalists call for recognition of the rights of nature. Human development requires the use of the services and resources provided by Earth's ecosystems, of course, but responsible use should endeavor to be caring and sustainable and avoid irreversible environmental harm. National legislation and international treaties protecting endangered species and conserving wildlife habitats, such as the Recovering America's Wildlife Act (RAWA) now before Congress, reflect the shift in attitude that is necessary.

In addition to the ethical and practical dimensions of the human relationship with nature, it is also important to appreciate the vital significance of people's spiritual experiences in and with nature. For millions of people, intimacy with nature is a major source of spiritual inspiration and artistic vision, awakening awe, wonder, enchantment, joy, a feeling of being part of a great sacred mystery, and inner peace. Relationships with animals and time in nature can be a source of emotional and spiritual healing. The beauty in nature can nurture a mystical intuition of a transcendent divine reality mysteriously present in and through all things, strengthening the love that drives the spiritual quest. The great creative and destructive forces at work in nature, over which human beings have no control and upon which they are dependent, teach respect for nature and humility regarding humanity's place in the grand scheme of things. The most moving spiritual experiences I had as a boy occurred in wild nature, which is the common experience of many young people. Providing opportunities to build relationships with nature should be part of any school program designed to support spiritual democracy. It can nurture and deepen a young person's spiritual growth and moral commitments.

Spiritual democracy in the twenty-first century calls for a holistic worldview supporting a relational spirituality that extends beyond its central focus on relations among people to encompass relationships with the larger whole, the totality, of which human beings are an interconnected part, and which includes the greater community of life on Earth and the evolving cosmos in all its infinite complexity. This means an American democratic culture that cultivates reverence for the mystery of being, a sense of belonging to the universe, gratitude for the gift of life, a love of Earth, and an ethical commitment to respect and care for the greater community of life and to practice sustainable development. Just as there can be tension between the needs of the individual and the needs of the human community so there is tension between the needs of the human community and the needs of the greater community of life. However, these tensions can be managed with the guidance of scientific research, new technologies, and a holistic and compassionate world view that appreciates the interconnectedness of all things and the sacredness of life.

An especially powerful symbol of the emerging integrated, holistic, global consciousness that views caring for people and caring for Earth as two interrelated aspects of one great task is the awe-inspiring image of Earth in the photographs taken by astronauts from space. This new consciousness is supported and deepened by the science-based story of the 13.8 billion-year unfolding of the universe and the emergence over the last 3 billion years of life on Earth.[27] The photographs of Earth from space and the universe story carry the message that our planet, the biosphere, life in all its diversity, human civilization, and democracy are interrelated, beautiful, fragile wonders, and with the gift of life and American citizenship goes a great responsibility to care for them and to strive for justice, the common good, and peace.

The diagram in Figure 2 on the following page outlines the different dimensions of the spiritual and ethical consciousness that this essay has associated with spiritual democracy for the twenty-first century. The dot in the center of the diagram represents the self and the rings extending outward represent the communities with which the self is interconnected and to which it belongs: families, local communities and organizations, the nation, the larger human family, the greater community of life, the planet, and beyond that the greater universe. The vertical lines of the cross represent the interdependence of the self and the community, recognizing that the self finds itself beyond itself and realizes its potential in and through caring, creative, intelligent relationships with the communities of which it is a part. The vertical lines of the cross indicate that meaning, purpose, and wellbeing are realized in and through the integration of the ideal and the real, the spiritual and the material, the sacred and the secular, the divine and the human.[28]

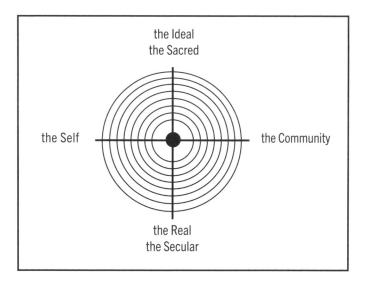

Fig. 2, The Spiritual and Ethical Consciousness Emerging
in the Twenty-First Century

It is also instructive to keep in mind that in the Christian tradition one interpretation of the symbolism of the Cross involves viewing it as representing the intersection of the eternal (the vertical section) with the temporal (the horizontal section). Eternity is not endless time. It is another dimension of reality to which human beings may awaken. The eternal may intersect with the temporal in deep spiritual experiences involving an expansion of consciousness and the awakening of compassion and love together with a profound sense of oneness, cosmic trust (faith in the meaning and value of life), and hope.

4

Democracy, Education, and Spirituality

The original American dream involves the vision of a new world in which people are free to pursue their dreams within a social environment that cultivates intelligent, responsible, engaged citizens with a compassionate concern for the dignity and rights of others and their general welfare, advancing the never-ending task of constructing "a more perfect Union." It is a vision of ideal possibilities that challenges society to keep expanding its ethical consciousness and concept of inclusive community and justice. The environmental crisis has added an ecological dimension to the unfolding social vision. Each generation is faced with the task of renewing its faith in the dream and constructing a fresh vision of the common good for the new age. In the twenty-first century, it should be central to the mission of the nation's schools to keep the original dream and its spirit alive, and toward that end to educate the whole child, mind, body, heart, and spirit, setting all young people on the path to authentic freedom, responsible democratic citizenship, and caring, creative leadership of their own lives and their communities.

Regarding the urgent need in this time of crisis for both institutional reform and cultural transformation, the PreK-12 schools are an especially critical part of American democracy's essential infrastructure. There is no better place to start the work of creating a culture of commitment to American constitutional democracy, to one another, to the greater community of life, and future generations. Childhood and adolescence are uniquely formative periods in the human life cycle, and it is hard to imagine how the nation can hope to reinvent American democracy for the twenty-first century without a transformation of schools that involves promoting education of the whole child and spiritual democracy. Moreover, achieving major change in America will take time, and preparing oncoming generations through the schools to carry this work forward is essential.

Charging the schools with supporting the moral and spiritual development of the nation's youth is not a new idea. It was widely held in the colonial era and throughout most of the nineteenth century that human development and a stable social order require morality and morality requires faith in God and religion. Communities looked to the schools as well as to families and institutional religion to tend the moral and spiritual foundations of society. In many homes and schools in the eighteenth and early nineteenth centuries, children were taught to read by studying the Bible. Beginning in the 1830s, state-supported "common schools" (public schools) were established by local governments with the understanding that they would ensure that young people acquire the knowledge, skills, and values to be good citizens. Spirituality and morality were closely associated with religion, and these schools were designed to inspire commitment to a Protestant Christian vision of basic, widely shared moral and spiritual ideals that its proponents argued were non-sectarian. However, with the ever-growing religious pluralism of American society, the increasing secularization of society, the spread of moral relativism, and vocal demands that schools respect constitutional provisions regarding the separation of church and state, it proved ever more difficult to develop and maintain a broad consensus on how public schools should support the spiritual and moral development of young people. Fierce debates and even violent conflicts have erupted over this issue. Nevertheless, the idea that the nation's schools should promote ethical values and character development has persisted.[29]

Beginning in the late nineteenth century and during the first half of the twentieth century, the progressive education movement, which was deeply influenced by the new developmental psychology and the emerging social sciences, focused special attention on the development of the whole child. In general, progressive education was characterized by a child-centered as opposed to a curriculum-centered approach, and its advocates were committed to creating schools that supported the social and political reforms being advanced by the broader Progressive Movement. While teaching at the University of Chicago in the 1890s, John Dewey was among the first educational reformers to create a laboratory school to generate the scientific knowledge needed to guide a transformation of schools with the goal of educating the whole child and advancing social reform. He was much concerned with the formation of a child's basic attitudes and values. However, in books like *The School and Society* (1901) and *Democracy and Education* (1915), he endeavored to find ways of addressing this challenge without involving organized religion, which he believed had come to divide rather than unify Americans. He envisioned schools becoming miniature communities governed by a unifying democratic spirit and the science-based art of forming in young people "fundamental dispositions, intellectual and moral, toward nature and fellow man."[30]

Dewey was the leading proponent of progressive education, but there were multiple innovative leaders and the movement influenced the practices in public schools as well as independent schools. However, as the nation emerged from World War II, the movement became fractured and lost its way. The scientific studies, creative experiments, and impassioned debates inspired by the movement remain an important influence in the ongoing evolution of educational reform in America, but progressive education ceased to be the banner under which reformers mobilized. Reflecting the influence of progressive education, the Universal Declaration of Human Rights adopted by the United Nations in 1947 calls for the education of the whole child with an emphasis on core democratic values. Article 26 states: "Education should be directed to the full development of the human personality and strengthening of respect for human rights and fundamental freedoms."

Two initiatives launched in Europe in the early twentieth century are especially noteworthy. The Montessori school movement, started in 1907 by the Italian physician, Maria Montessori, and the Waldorf school movement, initiated in 1919 in Germany by the philosopher, Rudolf Steiner, are prime examples of efforts to find creative new ways to educate the whole child. Both movements endeavor to support the intellectual, social, emotional, physical, moral, and spiritual dimensions of development, and today they operate hundreds of schools located in many countries including the United States. The motto of the Waldorf schools captures the spirit of these two innovative movements: "Accept the children with reverence. Educate them with love. Send them forth in freedom."[31]

By the 1960s and 70s, the vast majority of US public schools had been led to abandon a concern to nurture students' spiritual and moral formation. It is the association of spiritual and moral values and what is often called character education with religion that has made the issue especially controversial. The First Amendment to the Constitution adopted in 1791 prohibits the federal government from restricting the free exercise of religion or adopting laws that lead to an establishment of religion. In 1947, the Supreme Court made clear that the First Amendment applies to state and local governments and to public schools, which are operated by local governments, and that no tax dollars may be used to support religious activities or institutions. In the early 1960s, the Supreme Court ruled that any form of school prayer and school-sponsored religious instruction, including devotional Bible readings, is a violation of the First Amendment's prohibition against government establishment of religion. The Court's charge to the public schools is to provide a "secular education" that maintains a "strict and lofty neutrality as to religion." However, the Supreme Court has ruled that the academic study of the Bible and the history of religion is an important aspect of a well-rounded education and is permissible in public schools as part of a secular education program.[32]

Over the past two decades the most significant national efforts to reform the schools have focused largely on the curriculum, especially reading, writing, and math, and on the use of standardized tests to measure the progress of students, teachers, and schools. The No Child Left Behind Act of 2002 mandated annual testing in reading and math, but since there were no common standards and tests, the law was not very effective. In an effort to address this problem, in 2010, a bipartisan group of governors, state educational leaders, and school reformers designed and released the Common Core State Standards, which focuses on reading, writing, and math. Forty states adopted the Common Core State Standards, but opposition from groups on both the Left and the Right and a lack of teacher training and teaching materials has hampered implementation. The Every Student Succeeds Act of 2015 endeavored to update the No Child Left Behind Act with a strong emphasis on proficiency in tests. These initiatives have had some successes, but the performance of American students on international and national exams has not improved significantly, which reflects some serious problems with education in America. These exams, for example, indicate that two-thirds of American students are not proficient in reading. Further, in most public schools the emphasis on tests and test prepping has only narrowed the focus of teaching and learning.

This state of affairs, however, is not the whole story regarding the schools and spiritual and moral development over the past four decades. Many independent schools, some religious (Protestant, Roman Catholic, Jewish, etc.) and some secular have remained committed in a great variety of ways to supporting and nurturing the moral and spiritual life of their students. In addition, concerns over the unraveling of the moral fabric of American culture and the many problems with which young people struggle today, including mental health issues, over-exposure to social media, and underachievement in academic work, have led to renewed efforts to find acceptable secular ways to reform public school education and nurture moral and spiritual development. The following are among the most influential initiatives.

Reflecting the influence of the humanistic and transpersonal psychology movements in the 1980s, John Miller and Ron Miller launched the "holistic education" movement in the United States and Canada. "Holistic education," explains John Miller, "is about educating the whole person – body, mind, and spirit – within the context of an interconnected world."[33] The importance of spirituality in education is a central concern. Even though the term "holistic" education is relatively new, the theory and practice are not, asserts Miller. He cites the educational practices of Indigenous peoples and the great spiritual teachers from the Axial Age, including Confucius, Socrates, and Plato, and more recent philosophers of education such as Rousseau, Tolstoy, and the American Transcendentalists, as well as Steiner and Montessori, as educators who understood the vital importance of a holistic approach. The movement has created its own journal and inspired research projects and numerous books and conferences, attracting the support of thousands of teachers and activists in the United States, Canada, and many other countries. In the United States, almost all the major professional educational organizations have endorsed a focus on the whole child, even if the implementation of the goal remains unrealized. These organizations include the Association for Supervision and Curricular Development, the American Association of School Administrators, the National Association of Elementary School Principals, the National Association of Middle School Principals, and the National Association of Secondary School Principals.[34]

Among those educators and activists supportive of holistic education and spirituality in education are the many advocates for mindfulness in education. In recent decades, hundreds of public and charter schools across the country have adopted mindfulness-based programs (MBPs) for students and teachers. The core of these MBPs is a meditation practice that comes from Buddhism. However, the proponents of mindfulness in education argue that the practice can be disconnected from religion, and mindfulness is being promoted as a science-based, secular technique that supports stress reduction, mental health, and universal ethical virtues like compassion and loving-kindness. It is argued that contemporary studies in the field of neuroscience confirm its effectiveness as a source of well-being.

Buddhist teachers like the Dalai Lama, Thich Nhat Hanh, Jack Kornfield, and Sharon Salzberg have played a role in popularizing mindfulness meditation practices in America over the last forty years, but the influence of Jon Kabat-Zinn, a professor emeritus of medicine at the University of Massachusetts Medical School and a trained Buddhist dharma teacher, is especially significant. Kabat-Zinn designed, tested, and introduced Mindfulness-Based Stress Reduction (MBSR) in the 1980s at the Medical School, and it rapidly became "a model for innumerable MBPs in hospitals, public schools, prisons, government, media, professional sports, and business." Even though the idea for MBSR was initially inspired by Buddhist teachings and practices, Kabat-Zinn has promoted MBSR as a science-based approach to healing and well-being, not as a Buddhist religious discipline.[35]

Among those who encountered mindfulness through Kabat-Zinn's initiative is US Congressman Tim Ryan, (OH-13), who has become a committed advocate for public school MBPs. The title of his 2012 book, *A Mindful Nation: How A Simple Practice Can Help Us Reduce Stress, Improve Performance, and Recapture the American Spirit* expresses the profound significance that he and many others attribute to mindfulness and why they support its introduction into the nation's K-12 schools.[36] Organizations like MindUP, Mindful Schools, Calmer Choice, and Still Quiet Place have introduced mindfulness programs to many thousands of children in the US and internationally. The American Association for Mindfulness in Education (AME) is a collaborative supporting such organizations and the individuals who are training teachers and implementing MBPs in schools. AME asserts that "mindfulness practice does not depend on or interfere with any religion, cultural context, or belief system. Mindfulness can be completely secular." Even though studies of the brain and the impacts of MBPs in schools provide evidence of the benefits of mindfulness practices and one can adopt a mindfulness practice in pursuit of well-being as a religious person or non-religious person, there are some parents and teachers who ask whether Buddhist meditation practices and spiritual disciplines can be detached from their religious moorings and completely secularized. The mindfulness in education movement is a significant, promising development, but this question could become more of an issue in the years ahead as ever more schools adopt MBPs or other innovations that may be secularized versions of spiritual practices that have had religious connections. The support for mindfulness in education reflects the deep concern of growing numbers of Americans that the nation is adrift morally and spiritually and that schools must find new ways to provide young people with the support they desperately need.[37]

Over the past twenty-five years, the promotion of Social and Emotional Learning (SEL) has had a wide influence. The SEL movement has been led by the Collaborative for Academic, Social, and Emotional Learning (CASEL) and is supported by the National Commission on Social, Emotional, & Academic Development. The movement has been remarkably successful in making the argument that in addition to academic learning, social and emotional learning instills in young people knowledge, skills, and attitudes that are fundamental to their overall development, enhance their capacity for academic learning, and greatly strengthen their ability to feel and show empathy, build rewarding relationships, and work cooperatively with others. SEL focuses special attention on five areas: self-awareness; social awareness; self-management; relationship skills; and caring, responsible decision making. CASEL provides teachers with materials on curriculum, school culture, and class climate.

It has inspired a path-breaking initiative that is transforming the learning experience of thousands of young people in schools across America.[38]

Some leaders of the SEL movement have argued that the next step for SEL should be to support spirituality in education. Linda Lantieri, one of the founders of the SEL movement, makes such an argument in her book of essays, *Schools with Spirit: Nurturing the Inner Lives of Children and Teachers* (2001), and at a recent celebration of the 25th anniversary of the founding of CASEL, she again urged the movement to take on this challenge.[39] In a book welcomed by the holistic education movement, *The Soul of Education: Helping Students Find Connection, Compassion, and Character at School* (2000), Rachael Kessler, a teacher, SEL advocate, and founder of the PassageWorks Institute, presents a strong argument that schools need to address the spiritual dimension of their students' experience. In defending spirituality in public school education, she contends that an important distinction can be made between "ordinary experiences that can nourish spiritual development" and religious education and devotional practices. In addition, she understands the connection between spiritual development and democracy, stating: "If we are educating for wholeness, for citizenship, and leadership in a democracy, *spiritual development belongs in schools.*"[40] Kessler recognizes that both the well-being of young people and the renewal of American democracy require spirituality in education. In a recent speech at Teachers College, Columbia University, Timothy Shriver, CASEL board chair, spoke at length about the importance of spirituality in education. However, CASEL and the National Commission have not taken on this challenge directly, in all probability because of concerns that talk about spirituality in education will inevitably stir up old and new controversies over religion in education and could embroil CASEL in court challenges.[41]

Regarding education and the reinvention of American democracy, a major effort to renew and rebuild civic education and the teaching of American history is underway, which provides a unique opportunity to support spiritual democracy in and through the schools. By the beginning of the twenty-first century, civic education across the country had fallen into a state of neglect. In 2009, Supreme Court Justice Sandra Day O'Connor endeavored to reverse the trend by founding iCivics, a bipartisan initiative that has become the leading national organization promoting civic education and designing and distributing related educational materials that are now going to thousands of teachers and over 7.5 million students. To build a national movement, in 2018 iCivics formed CivXNow, a coalition of over 130 organizations that support the renewal of civic education.[42]

A recent publication of iCivics provides a new innovative and ambitious resource for teaching civics and American history, "Roadmap to Educating for American Democracy" (EAD), funded by the National Endowment for the Humanities and the US Department of Education. The "Roadmap" is in part an endeavor to act on the recommendations on education set forth in the National Commission report, "Our Common Purpose: Reinventing American Democracy for the 21st Century." The introduction to the "Roadmap" states:

> In recent decades, we as a nation have failed to prepare young Americans for self-government, leaving the world's oldest constitutional democracy in grave danger, afflicted by both cynicism and nostalgia, as it approaches its 250th anniversary. The time has come to recommit to the education of our young people for informed, authentic, and engaged citizenship. Our civic strength requires excellent civic and history education to repair the foundations of our democratic republic...Just as we invested in STEM education in response to the Cold War, the Sputnik moment, and the economic challenges of globalization, now in response to our dysfunction and failures of governance we need an equivalent scale of investment for civic learning.[43]

Over the next ten years, iCivics and its collaborators aspire to train 1 million K-12 teachers and to transmit to 60 million students in 100,000 schools "the knowledge, skills, and civic virtues" essential to becoming caring, engaged, constructive American citizens in the 21st century. The initiative is designed to promote "a love and understanding of constitutional democracy," and among the virtues it emphasizes are reflective patriotism, civil disagreement, and civic friendship.[44]

Regarding the teaching of American history, the "Roadmap" does not attempt to establish a new set of national standards or to provide a new curriculum. Instead, it adopts "an inquiry-based approach" and sets forth a host of carefully constructed questions for teachers and students at different grade levels (K-2, 3-5, 6-8, and 9-12) that will lead them to explore crucial issues related to seven broad themes. It also identifies five design challenges for state and local education leaders and teachers faced with the task of constructing a curriculum.[45] With this approach, it endeavors to identify the major issues and provide guidance without taking set positions on the most contentious matters in current partisan debates over just what and how schools should teach about slavery and racism in America and other controversial topics. Surveys indicate that there is wide public support for civic education, and iCivics and the CivXNow Coalition have succeeded in building bipartisan support in Congress for the Civics Secures Democracy Act, which if adopted, would provide states and districts major financial support for expanded programs in civics and U.S. history.

Louise Dube, who heads iCivics, and other leaders of the civics education movement have released a statement on "Spirituality and the Common Good," calling for education in the nation's schools that "nurtures not only the minds but also the hearts and spirits of young people." The statement affirms that "at the heart of the American experiment" are "spiritual ideals," and it asserts that civic education involves a "distinctly spiritual endeavor." Using one of Abraham Lincoln's phrases, the co-signers state: "We understand the goal of civic education to be the awakening and nurturing of the better angels of our nature."[46] The educational movement to help renew American democracy that iCivics is leading and the "EAD Roadmap" are promising initiatives with significant institutional support that could have a major positive impact on the values and thinking of emerging generations of young Americans. There is already collaboration between iCivics and the SEL movement. If spiritual democracy is the inspiration and true foundation of American democracy, it should be the foundation of any program that endeavors to advance civic education. It remains to be seen whether and how the civic education movement will actively and fully support education for the whole child, natural spirituality, and the vision and values set forth in "Spirituality and the Common Good."

Over the past 25 years, Lisa Miller's path-breaking research in the field of psychology and spirituality has established her as the leading psychologist on the protective benefits of spirituality for children, adolescents, and adults. She is many things: a clinical psychologist and research scientist; professor of psychology and education at Teachers College, Columbia University; author of two books and numerous publications in professional journals; consultant on spiritual preparedness with the US military; wife and mother; and an individual with roots in the Jewish tradition on her own spiritual journey. In 2015, Miller published *The Spiritual Child: The New Science on Parenting for Health and Lifelong Thriving*, which sets forth for a wide audience the findings of her collaborative research in the fields of psychology and neuroscience on the spiritual life of children and adolescents.[47]

The book presents an especially compelling argument in support of education for the whole child in PreK-12 schools, emphasizing the vital importance of strengthening the deep inner core of children and nurturing their capacity for spiritual development. Her research provides hard evidence that children are born as spiritual beings as well as social and moral beings. They are equipped at birth with innate spiritual capacities that reflect

their genetic makeup, but the cultural environment and socialization have a major influence on how these inborn capacities are
developed. Further, regarding the protective benefits of spirituality, her research demonstrates that when the innate spiritual capacities of children and adolescents are supported and nurtured,
they are more likely to do well academically and much less likely
than others to be overcome by anxiety and depression and to be
at risk for alcoholism, drug abuse, other harmful behaviors, and
suicide. In general, they are more likely to be resilient, thrive, and
develop rewarding relationships and meaningful careers. Miller
writes that there are now hundreds of peer-reviewed scientific
articles that show "inborn spirituality as foundational to mental
health and wellness, particularly as it develops in the first two
decades...Spiritual development is for our species a biological
and psychological imperative at birth." "The data suggests," she
also explains, "that it is much easier and more likely for adults to
be spiritual if that sense is fostered during childhood and adolescence."[48] These findings are a wakeup call for America regarding
what the well-being of the nation's young people requires of parents, religious institutions, and schools and what schools must
do to help create the spiritually mature and morally responsible
leaders and citizens the nation so desperately needs in business,
civil society, politics, government, and the military as well as in
family life.

The same year her book came out, Miller launched the National
Council on Spirituality in Education with a conference at Teachers College that attracted over 350 heads of school, teachers, and
educational reformers. Two years later, Miller became the founding president of the Collaborative for Spirituality in Education
(CSE), a not-for-profit organization based at Teachers College
and established to support her ongoing research and leadership
with the financial support of the Fetzer Institute. (Disclosure: I
am the co-chair of the CSE board of trustees.) With the support of CSE, the National Council on Spirituality in Education
provides an ongoing forum for the sharing of new research, suc-

cessful innovations, and promising new ideas. What is especially significant is that Professor Miller's vision for a transformation of the schools is science-based. It is the new science regarding natural spirituality that is changing the debate about whether and how to promote the spiritual development of young people in America's public and independent schools.

In 2021, Miller published a second and more detailed account of her research, *The Awakened Brain: The New Science of Spirituality and Our Quest for an Inspired Life*, to which we will return. First, it is instructive to consider some developments in the fields of psychology and philosophy regarding religion and spirituality, which will help to deepen our understanding of natural spirituality and spiritual democracy.

5

Science, Religion, and Natural Spirituality

In 1901 and 1902, William James, the Harvard University psychologist and philosopher, delivered in Edinburgh, Scotland, his pathbreaking Gifford Lectures on Natural Religion, which were published as *The Varieties of Religious Experience: A Study in Human Nature*. The interest in "natural religion" can be traced back to the European Enlightenment in the eighteenth century, and the concept fascinated thinkers like Thomas Jefferson. Under the influence of the mathematical and mechanistic interpretation of nature in Newtonian science, the natural was equated with the rational. The Enlightenment concept of natural religion was, therefore, linked with the idea of rational religion and the endeavor to use reason and the test of social utility to identify those fundamental beliefs thought to constitute the essence of true religion such as the belief in an omnipotent divine Creator, a cosmic moral order, and immortality. This eighteenth-century concept of natural or rational religion was focused primarily on defending basic beliefs thought to be both consistent with Newtonian science and essential to sustaining the moral order of society. Interest in the concept faded in the nineteenth century, but a concern to find a way to reconcile religion and science kept alive in some quarters the idea of natural religion.[49] James rejected the eighteenth-century idea that the essence of religion can be reduced to a set of rational beliefs, and he became passionately engaged in developing a very different understanding of religious faith.

James was far more influenced by Darwinian biology and evolutionary theory than Newtonian mathematics and mechanics, and he had abandoned interest in the Neo-Hegelian philosophical endeavor to harmonize religious belief with modern science by appealing to grand, speculative, metaphysical visions. For the purposes of his study, he defines religion as involving the relationship of individuals "to whatever they may consider the divine," recognizing that the idea of the divine can take different forms. In addition, as a psychologist who had recently published a path-breaking work on *The Principles of Psychology*, he adopts an empirical method of analysis and focuses on developing an understanding of the origin, nature, and function of "personal religion," that is, individual religious experience, which he distinguishes from institutional religion. He is especially concerned to emphasize that direct, immediate experiences in the form of mystical intuitions and emotions, not reason, are the wellspring and real source of religious faith and the heart of religion. Creeds, theological systems, and the philosophy of religion are secondary phenomena that arise with the need to interpret religious experience and clarify and defend religious beliefs.[50]

His analysis of the varieties of religious experience as they have appeared in diverse cultures and religions convinced him that they have "a common nucleus," which is revealed most clearly in their more profound and intense manifestations. He contends that religious experiences, which lead to what he calls the "faith-state," come as a gift but they engage inborn, natural human capacities. Further, they have a highly significant biological and psychological function essential to human well-being involving a distinctive, positive transformation in people's way of being, their state of mind and attitude in relation to life and the world.[51]

James makes an important distinction between the personal religion of the healthy-minded, who view the natural world as basically good and live with an optimistic faith in progress, and the religion of the sick soul, who has been overwhelmed by pessimism, fear, and despair in the face of evil, sin, suffering, and death.[52] That the faith-state can liberate the sick soul from despair, awakening a profound sense of light and love flowing from a higher power, generating trust in the meaning and value of life, restoring the yes to life, instilling "enthusiastic gladness" and inner peace, as well as "a preponderance of loving affections in relation to others," this is for James clear indication of the vital importance of religious experience for human wellbeing. Having analyzed at length Leo Tolstoy's struggle with death and despair and his spiritual awakening, James endorses Tolstoy's assertion that "Faith… is the force whereby we live." With the sick soul in mind, James adds: "The total absence of it …means collapse." The inborn capacity for spiritual experience, he states, is a vitally important "human faculty," "an essential organ of our life, performing a function which no other portion of our nature can so successfully fulfill."[53] His research leads him to "the conclusion that a man's [personal] religion is the deepest and wisest thing in his life."[54]

James was convinced that "our normal waking consciousness, rational consciousness as we call it, is but one special type of consciousness, whilst all about it, parted from it by the filmiest of screens, there lies – potential forms of consciousness entirely different." Moreover, he concludes that the mystical intuitions, feelings, and insights that form the core of religious experience arise from a "more profound part of our nature" than "the loquacious level which rationalism inhabits."[55] In this regard, he argues that "the existence of mystical states absolutely overthrows the pretension of non-mystical states to be the sole and ultimate dictators of what we may believe." James believed in science, but he forcefully rejected scientism. What religious experience and the faith-state "unequivocally testifies to is that we can experience union with something larger than ourselves and in that union find our greatest peace," asserts James. He takes seriously the idea that the visible world may be part of a more spiritual universe, and he leaves open the possibility that the religious dimension of experience may involve a relationship with God, a transcendent divine power.[56]

Responding to some of his critics, James observes that many highly educated people in the academic world put too much trust in reason and science as the only path to truth and as a result suffer from "paralysis of their native capacity for faith," which he views as a form of "mental weakness." The implication of James' thinking about the vital importance of the faith state is that if there were to be widespread paralysis of the innate capacity for spiritual awakening and awareness in a society, its people would be at risk for psychological and social breakdown. It is important, however, to make clear that James' appreciative analysis of the nature and function of individual religious experience did not reflect an uncritical view of institutional religion. He argues that organized religion needs far greater respect for reason and science and should abandon beliefs that are "scientifically absurd or incongruous."[57]

James' brilliant, complex, in-depth study remains a major contribution to the psychology and philosophy of religion. His call for the scientific study of religious experience, the distinction between personal religious experience and institutional religion, and his view of mystical intuition and faith as a "native capacity" and source of wisdom and happiness contributed to a growing interest in the study of spirituality. Over the course of the next century, this would lead to the emergence of the psychology of spirituality as a distinct field of scientific inquiry with important implications for education. Instead of talking about natural religion, psychologists would begin to discuss natural spirituality and make a distinction between spirituality and religion.

During the first five or six decades of the twentieth century, a growing number of psychologists and philosophers would come to focus their study of religion on religious experience, especially mysticism, as distinct from the beliefs, creeds, rituals, and organizational structures of institutional religion that interest anthropologists and sociologists. The work of Evelyn Underhill, Carl Jung, Rudolf Otto, Henri Bergson, and Walter Stace are examples. In addition, during the first half of the twentieth century, there were thinkers in the academic world who rejected belief in God and institutional religion but who valued certain forms of religious experience, including piety toward nature, a sense of belonging to the universe, cosmic trust, reverence for life, compassion, and a concern for social justice. They regarded themselves as "religious humanists." A number of them together with John Dewey signed "A Humanist Manifesto" in 1933. Among the humanists who supported the human potential movement during the 1960s, 70s, and 80s there was much interest in various forms of religious experience as contributing to human self-realization and well-being. Experimentation with psychedelic drugs like LSD was an important influence in the widening discussion. Moreover, the interest in religious experience as potentially transformative and liberating was a major reason for the explosion of interest in Buddhist and Hindu forms of meditation, the practice of mindfulness, yoga, and other Eastern religious disciplines that occurred in America and other Western societies during and following the 1960s. For most of the century, spiritual experiences were generally considered to be an aspect of the religious dimension of experience and were labeled "religious" experiences regardless of whether they occurred in the context of religion.

The wide interest in and study of "religious" experience did generate an increasing focus on spirituality as a distinct sphere of inquiry within the field of religious studies. For example, in the 1980s and 90s over 500 scholars contributed essays to a twenty-five-volume series on spirituality and the world's religions entitled *World Spirituality: An Encyclopedic History of the Religious Quest*. The series is designed "to present the spiritual wisdom of the human race in its unfolding" from prehistoric times to the present. The many scholars involved in the project did not agree on one common definition of spirituality. However, in "The Preface to the Series," the purpose of the project is explained as follows:

The series focuses on that inner dimension of the person called by certain traditions "the spirit." This spiritual core is the deepest center of the person. It is here that the person is open to the transcendent dimension: it is here that the person experiences ultimate reality. The series explores the discovery of this core, the dynamics of its development, and its journey to the ultimate goal.[58]

The publication of the *World Spirituality* series reflects the expanding and deepening encounter and dialogue among the world's religions that took place during the last four decades of the twentieth century. In this regard, "The Preface to the Series" concludes with the following observation: "It may well be that the meeting of spiritual paths – the assimilation not only of one's own spiritual heritage but of that of the human community as a whole – is the distinctive spiritual journey of our time." This is a hopeful vision. The sharing and assimilation of the spiritual wisdom of the human community as a whole could be of incalculable benefit as humanity endeavors to find its way to a promising future. It has already helped schools as they search for spiritual practices like mindfulness that can be adapted for use with young people in secular education programs.

The *World Spirituality* series presents the history of spirituality as primarily a story about the development of the world's religions and as fundamental to understanding the religious quest. However, one volume in the series, *Spirituality and the Secular Quest*, which was published in 1996, asserts that "being religious is not a necessary condition for being spiritual" and there can be "a spiritual dimension in secular activities." With a primary focus on Western societies, the essays explore various forms of "secular spirituality," that is, diverse ways people find "spiritual meaning in secular activities."[59]

As the overview in this essay indicates, in the course of the twentieth-century thinkers studying religious experience and spirituality have identified various ways in which a person can be spiritual without being religious, that is, without being involved in institutional religion. Different types of secular spirituality, including some brands of ethical or religious humanism, such as Dewey's philosophy of religious experience, are examples. Over the past three decades, a number of psychologists have also emphasized the further observation that people can be religious without being spiritual. Institutional religion and spirituality are often closely interrelated, they assert, but they are not identical. This is not a novel idea, but it has gained a new wide acceptance. In contemporary surveys, for example, some Americans identify themselves as religious but not spiritual, while others identify as spiritual and religious or as spiritual but not religious. As this way of thinking has taken hold, ordinary people, as well as scholars, are more likely to refer to "spiritual" experience rather than "religious" experience, especially when talking about spiritual experiences that occur outside the framework of religion such as spiritual perceptions generated by encounters with nature or deep feelings of meaning and purpose awakened by engagement in social movements.

In this connection, a new field of scientific research has emerged in recent decades focused on psychology and spirituality, and it gives special attention to spiritual development in the life of children and adolescents. There are connections between the new science and the earlier work done in the psychology of religion, but the new science is not focused primarily on religion. Its focus is on what some psychologists call natural spirituality, a concept with a broader meaning than secular spirituality. In 2012, Professor Lisa Miller edited and published *The Oxford Handbook on Psychology and Spirituality* with an extensive collection of essays that provide an overview of the emerging field.[60] *The new science emphasizes that quite apart from any religion every child is born with a natural capacity for spiritual development. Moreover, this universal, innate capacity is understood to be an integral dimension of overall human development that provides a vitally important foundation of resilience, meaning, and purpose for a young person's cognitive, emotional, social, and moral development. Further, this inborn capacity can be nurtured both within and apart from institutional religion.*

What inspired the creation of the world's great religious traditions is the spiritual experience of their founders, and for countless numbers of people spirituality is the true heart of religion and religious practices provide them with the most effective way to nurture and cultivate the spiritual life. It is also the case that many people associate being religious with right belief and active participation in the external forms of religion, including obedience to a moral code, but they have little interest in nurturing their inner life and growing spiritually. This description can be applied to some religious conservatives and some religious liberals. There are deep connections between spirituality and the history of institutional religion, but there is also a distinction to be made between spirituality and religion. Regarding public schools, since spirituality and religion are not identical and natural spirituality can be nurtured both within and outside the framework of religion, it should be possible for schools to find ways to support and nurture the spiritual development of young people without promoting or opposing institutional religion.

In seeking to understand and appreciate current efforts to argue that spirituality can be nurtured apart from religion, it is instructive to remember that over the centuries there have been a number of philosophers, mystics, artists, poets, and novelists who have celebrated spiritual experience, explored the psychology of spirituality, and promoted spiritual growth apart from organized religion. Their insights remain profoundly relevant to the contemporary discussion about natural spirituality and the concept of spiritual democracy supported in this essay.

Socrates and Plato, the founders of the liberal arts tradition in education, are prime examples. Almost 2,500 years ago, they taught that the matter of supreme importance in life is care for one's soul and that the primary purpose of education, especially the education of future leaders, should be the search for wisdom and the cultivation of virtue. They identified the soul with reason, but they defined reason broadly to include the power of direct, spiritual (*noetic*) insight as well as the capacity for logical thinking. People naturally desire the good, in the sense of happiness and fulfillment, taught Socrates. The problem is that almost everyone is ignorant of what constitutes well-being, the good. What makes things worse is that people tend to be ignorant of their ignorance. As a consequence, even though they seek the good they are misguided in their pursuit of it. They are imprisoned in their delusions. The true good and key to happiness is wisdom, being possessed by a knowledge of the good, which involves learning from experience, searching rational inquiry, and deep spiritual insight. The profoundest insights involve recovering truth buried deep within the soul, believed Socrates and Plato. People confuse the true source of happiness with having wealth, power, fame, and pleasure. These things can contribute to a person's well-being and happiness, but without wisdom people do not know how to manage them well, leading to endless problems, conflicts, and much suffering.

Plato transformed the supernatural realm of the gods into a world of eternal truths and ideals. He considered the highest forms of spiritual practice to be the search for wisdom through philosophical dialogue and contemplation of the True, the Beautiful, and the Good, which he identified with Being itself, the sacred source of all that is. For those with the necessary intellectual and spiritual gifts, the goal is a mystical enlightenment. In Plato's dialogues, when Socrates leads people to recognize and confess their state of ignorance, it both humbles them and awakens a passion for self-knowledge and wisdom. This intense desire to be one with the Beautiful and the Good is the deeper meaning of the love Plato labeled *eros*. This innate yearning for wholeness drives the spiritual quest.[61]

Inspired by Socratic teachings, the Stoic philosophers regarded philosophical reflection and dialogue as a spiritual practice. Just as medicine was thought to provide a cure for the body, philosophy was considered a cure for the soul. The Stoics' spiritual approach and worldview, including their insights regarding freedom and their defense of universal human values, had a profound impact on the attitude toward life of many people in the Roman empire, and their philosophy of life has had a lasting influence. One of the primary sources inspiring Christian mysticism are the writings of Plotinus, a Neo-Platonic philosopher from the Hellenistic period. He taught that the entire universe emanates from the Eternal One, the Absolute Good, like light radiating from the sun. The One is ineffable, an undifferentiated unity transcending all conceptualization. Not a being among the other beings that make up the universe, the One is the sacred power of being immanent within every person and all things, interconnecting all that is. Enlightenment involves a journey inward leading to a mystical experience of union with the One.

One criticism leveled against the Socratic view that ignorance and delusion are the fundamental spiritual problem, an outlook shared by Buddhism, is the argument that people often know very well what they should do to advance their wellbeing and the good of the community, but they do not do it. In defense of Socrates' position, there is a critical distinction to be made between knowing and knowing. A purely intellectual, head-centered form of knowing often has no influence over a person's desires and behavior. What is required to transform a person's character and actions is experiential insight that engages a person's whole being, the heart, and feeling as well as the mind. Achieving wisdom goes beyond acquiring information and trying to grasp the truth with one's reason. It involves an encounter with the living truth and being grasped by the truth in the core of one's being.

Arthur Miller, the playwright, explained in an interview that when writing a play that grapples with a critical moral issue like anti-Semitism his intent is not to instruct the audience with rational arguments and explanations, which will have limited impact. His objective is to create on stage a drama that makes the people "see with their guts." Effective spiritual teachers use parables and stories as well as deep dialogue to awaken transformative spiritual and moral understanding rather than abstract rational arguments. In his short story about the dynamics of a spiritual awakening, *The Death of Ivan Ilyich*, Leo Tolstoy comments that Ivan Ilyich readily accepted, as most people would, the rational conclusion of the syllogism, "Kai is a man. All men die. Therefore, Kai will die." However, Ivan never really understood and believed that this truth applied to him personally until he was gripped by a mortal illness. When that happened, it precipitated an emotional and spiritual crisis that was the beginning of a spiritual transformation, leading him from a self-centered existence, darkness, and despair to compassion, light, and joy.[62]

6

To Have and To Be

Among a number of twentieth and twenty-first-century psychologists and philosophers with a special interest in the spiritual life, a major theme in their writing is a distinction between two fundamentally different attitudes toward life or ways of being. The distinction they make in this regard is consistent with the teachings in the great spiritual traditions that warn against delusion and selfishness and call for wisdom, compassion, and self-giving love. However, their thought involves some illuminating contemporary formulations. The title of Erich Fromm's book, *To Have or To Be?*, identifies the core issue, which has profound implications for an understanding of spiritual democracy and the purpose of education. In this connection, it is instructive to consider the thought of Martin Buber, Viktor Frankl, the Dalai Lama, and Jonathan Haidt as well as Erich Fromm and Lisa Miller.

Martin Buber's reflections and meditations in *I and Thou (Ich und Du)*, which has been described as a philosophic poem, was published in 1923 and has come to be one of the most influential twentieth-century writings on the spiritual life. Buber was centrally concerned with generating a renewal of Judaism by recovering the original and true spirit of the tradition. In this regard, he focuses on spirituality, not rituals and observances, and for him, spirituality is all about realizing the deeper meaning and true fullness of life in and through authentic relationships and building community. Buber was also concerned to address the spiritual crisis gripping Western civilization, which he believed had lost all genuine sense of the sacred, and his I–Thou philosophy, which he labeled biblical humanism, struck a chord with people from other traditions, especially Christianity. In addition, as the philosopher and translator of *I and Thou*, Walter Kaufman, comments, Buber's vision "speaks to those who no longer believe but who wonder whether life without religion is bound to lack some dimension," and it "appeals to that religiousness which finds no home in organized religion."[63]

Central to Buber's philosophy is a distinction between two different attitudes and ways of relating to the world, which he designates with the word pairs I-It and I-Thou.[64] When a person interacts with the world with the attitude of I-It, people, other living beings, and all other things are viewed and treated as objects to be analyzed, possessed, controlled, and used. In this connection, Buber writes: "In all seriousness of truth, listen: without It a human being cannot live. But whoever lives only with that is not human." Every person is born with a yearning for authentic relationship. It is in and through realizing this innate capacity to relate to other persons and all life as a Thou that human beings discover the deeper meaning and purpose of life, asserts Buber. An I-Thou relationship requires the engagement of a person's whole being and involves being wholeheartedly present with and for the other. "Nothing conceptual intervenes between I and You." Such relationships are the expression of the spirit of compassion and love and are the source of true community. Buber asserts that I-Thou encounters are the product of both "will and grace." Regarding the role of grace, it is helpful to keep in mind that deep aesthetic and spiritual experiences cannot, like falling in love, be had by willing them. One must prepare oneself and be open to them, but they involve being taken from beyond oneself. Buber also contends that I-Thou encounters awaken "intimations of eternity." One encounters God, the Eternal Thou, not by turning away from the world, but in and through I-Thou relationships with other persons, the greater community of life, and the living spirit of creative ideas.[65] In Buber's understanding,

God transcends the realm of I-It and one may never have an I-It relationship with God, but in and through the events of everyday life a person who is spiritually awake may encounter the divine presence and be addressed by the Eternal Thou.

Buber's overarching objective is to promote a relational spirituality designed to help people living in the modern world realize the deeper meaning and spiritual possibilities of everyday life, overcoming the separation of the spiritual and the material, the sacred and the secular. His world-affirming vision gives expression to spiritual insights and a natural spirituality essential to human wellbeing that can be supported and practiced both within and apart from organized religion. Buber's concept of an I-Thou relationship can be understood as an attempt to describe the deeper forms of what Dewey had in mind when he writes about democracy "as a life of free and enriching communion" and celebrates "the mystic force...of communication, the miracle of shared life and shared experience." There are many differences in Buber's and Dewey's approaches as philosophers but they both aspired to integrate the spiritual dimension of experience and everyday life, emphasizing the kind of transformative relationships that build and sustain liberating, thriving human communities.

In *Man's Search for Meaning*, Viktor Frankl, the psychotherapist and spiritual philosopher, also endeavors to envision a natural spirituality that integrates spiritual life and everyday life. The book provides a vivid account of his experience as a prisoner in a Nazi concentration camp during World War II. What Frankl came to realize and endeavored to help his fellow prisoners grasp is that the last and best protection against being overwhelmed by a sense of meaninglessness, depression, and despair in the midst of the horrors of the Nazi death camps was the awakening of spiritual awareness. "What was really needed was a fundamental change in our attitude toward life," writes Frankl. "We had to learn ourselves and, furthermore, we had to teach the despairing men, that *it did not really matter what we expected from life, but rather what life expected from us*."[66] What Frankl learned is that by turning around the basic question with which we face life, shifting the focus from me to we, and responding to life with care and compassion, it is possible to find a sustaining sense of meaning and purpose even in the midst of great injustice and suffering. Frankl believed that life eventually confronts all human beings with this fundamental issue and all have the inborn capacity to turn around the basic question with which they approach life quite apart from whether they are involved in organized religion. As a psychotherapist, he viewed a radical change in one's attitude toward life as the foundation of mental health and human well-being. Turning the question around is the central issue in natural spirituality and spiritual democracy.

The psychoanalyst and social philosopher, Erich Fromm, came to appreciate the wisdom in the thought of the world's great spiritual teachers, and in *To Have or To Be?* (1976) he endeavors to construct a "radical humanism" that recognizes the vital importance for modern society of spiritual development and a relational spirituality, which he argues can be cultivated without depending on religion. His conceptual framework in this regard can be very helpful in explaining the meaning of natural spirituality and spiritual democracy in a secular context. Fromm is centrally concerned with the realization of the human potential and with what constitutes authentic freedom and wellbeing, and with this objective guiding the inquiry, the book is "an analysis of selfishness and altruism as two basic character orientations." Fromm identifies "character orientation" with a person's or group's way of being, that is, the values, attitudes, and beliefs that form the true motivation governing their behavior. "Our being is the reality, the spirit that moves us, the character that impels our behavior," he writes. A person's character orientation reflects the state of the individual's deep inner core, the heart. His book is about the urgent need in Western societies for "a radical change of the human heart."[67]

Fromm argues that human beings are faced with a choice between two fundamentally different character orientations that shape the way they relate to self and the world and go about the pursuit of happiness, one centered around having more and the other committed to being more. One involves character traits that are "pathogenic and eventually produce a sick person, and thus, a sick society."[68] The other, argues Fromm, is the only path to enduring individual wellbeing and a healthy participatory democracy, justice, and the common good.

People with a having character orientation are egocentric and find their identity in what they possess, own, control, and use for their own self-centered ends and personal happiness understood as maximum pleasure. It is, of course, necessary to have things in order to survive and advance human well-being. However, "in the having mode of existence, my relationship to the world is... one in which I want to make everybody and everything, including myself, into my property."[69] What Fromm is describing is similar to what Buber identified as the I-It mode of existence. Everything is reduced to its utilitarian value. Fromm emphasizes that a people's character orientation and the socioeconomic structure of society are interdependent, mutually reinforcing, and the emphasis on private property, profit-making, and consumerism in modern industrial-technological societies tends to support and promote the having orientation.

People with a character orientation committed to being more, find their identity in growing intellectually, emotionally, morally, and spiritually and in cultivating their innate human capacities for experiential insight, understanding, caring, relating, creating, giving, sharing, loving, and serving. Such a way of being requires self-knowledge, inner freedom, and independence of thought.

> Its fundamental characteristic is that of activity, not in the sense of outward activity, of busyness, but inner activity, the productive use of our human powers. To be active means to give expression to one's faculties, talents, to the wealth of human gifts with which - though in varying degrees – every human being is endowed. It means to renew oneself, to grow,

to flow out, to give, to love, to transcend the prison of one's isolated ego..."[70]

Fromm asserts that both the having and the being character orientations are innate tendencies and natural potentialities of human nature. The biological need to survive tends to promote the having mode. However, there is also in human nature "an inherent and deeply rooted desire to be: to express our faculties, to be active, to be related to others, to escape the prison cell of selfishness...to share, to give, to sacrifice."[71] In this connection, Fromm writes:

> The human desire to experience union with others is rooted in the specific conditions of existence that characterize the human species and is one of the strongest motivators of human behavior. By the combination of minimal instinctive determination and maximal development of the capacity for reason, we human beings have lost our original oneness with nature. In order not to feel utterly isolated – which would, in fact, condemn us to insanity – we need to find a new unity with our fellow beings and with nature...The desire to experience union with others manifests itself in the lowest kind of behavior, i.e., in acts of sadism and destruction, as well as in the highest: solidarity on the basis of an ideal or conviction...Crucial to every society is the kind of union and solidarity it fosters.[72]

Spiritual democracy is about the nature and quality of the spirit of "union and solidarity" that society and its groups and institutions cultivate. This cultivation begins in homes, schools, and religious communities.

Fromm concludes that we human beings must decide which of the two basic innate potentials in human nature we want to govern our personalities and cultivate, keeping in mind that enduring change requires transforming both the dominant culture of a society and the character structure of individuals. Writing in the 1970s, he calls for a "conversion to a humanistic 'religiosity'." In his vision for the future of humanity, like that of Buber and Dewey, "social life itself – in all its aspects in work, in leisure, in personal relations – will be the expression of the 'religious' spirit."[73] Given the existence of nuclear weapons and current social, economic, and environmental trends, Fromm warns that the survival of the human species hinges on our capacity to bring about such change.

Among those promoting the idea that natural spirituality can be cultivated apart from religion is one of the world's best-known and most influential religious leaders, the XIVth Dalai Lama. His thinking in this regard is set forth in a book on spirituality and universal ethics, *Beyond Religion: Ethics for a Whole World*, published in 2011.[74] While acknowledging the extraordinary progress that humanity has made in the modern era, including the spread of the ideals of freedom, human rights, and democracy, he argues that given the persistence of widespread poverty, social injustice, violent conflict, and environmental degradation, something fundamental is missing in industrial – technological societies. The underlying problem is, he asserts, the neglect of spirituality and inner values. Shared ethical values are urgently needed to guide and govern human development. Reflecting on the diversity of religious faiths, the conflicts that can arise among them, and the declining influence of religion in Western societies and elsewhere, he concludes that in our contemporary multicultural societies one cannot look to religion to provide a basis for promoting universal values.[75]

The Dalai Lama, therefore, proposes "a new secular approach" to spirituality and universal ethics. However, he is careful to reject Western ideas of secularism that conceive it as opposed to religion. He supports a brand of secularism that supports "mutual tolerance and respect for all faiths as well as for those of no faith." His objective is a way to understand and cultivate spiritual values "without contradicting any religion and yet, crucially, without depending on religion." *Beyond Religion* endeavors to set forth "a genuinely sustainable and universal approach to ethics, inner values, and personal integrity – an approach that can transcend religious, cultural, and racial differences and appeal to people at a fundamental human level." He describes it "as a natural and rational" approach.[76]

Spirituality has two distinct dimensions explains the Dalai Lama: "our basic human spirituality (natural spirituality), which is the source of "basic spiritual wellbeing," and "religion-based spirituality," which is the product of socialization. Natural spirituality "does not depend on religion but comes from our innate human nature as beings with a natural disposition toward compassion, kindness, and caring for others." This "core disposition toward compassion" is "a natural instinct, bequeathed to us by our biological nature." Compassion involves empathy, identifying with the suffering of others, but goes beyond empathy. It is the "desire to alleviate the suffering of others and to promote their well-being." It is the spiritual principle from which all the other "positive inner qualities of the human heart" emerge, including kindness, patience, honesty, self-discipline, cooperation, tolerance, forgiveness, generosity, and justice. "Compassion is a marvel of human nature, a precious inner resource, and the foundation of our wellbeing and the harmony of our communities," declares the Dalai Lama. "We start to live spiritually," he explains, when we actively begin to nurture and cultivate our instinct for compassion and at the same time strive to constrain the destructive emotional tendencies, like anger and hatred, that are also inherent in human nature. These spiritual practices do not necessarily require religion even though many people find religion very beneficial in this regard.[77]

The Dalai Lama notes that the existence of compassion as an inborn instinct is confirmed today by contemporary scientific research in the fields of neuroscience and psychology. He also finds that evolutionary biology is helping to explain its origins. Human nature with its disposition toward compassion has evolved to reflect the reality that human beings can only survive and thrive in a social environment that supports kindness and cooperation. When discussing the need to cultivate one's spiritual growth, he distinguishes two levels of compassion.

> The first is the biological level...exemplified by the affection of a mother for her newborn child. The second is the extended level which has to be deliberately cultivated. While compassion at the biological level can be unconditional like the mother's love for her baby, it is also biased and limited in scope. Nevertheless, it is of the utmost importance because it is the seed from which unbiased compassion can grow. We can take our innate capacity for warmheartedness and, using our intelligence and conviction, expand it.[78]

It is the deepening awareness of our common humanity, he explains, that can awaken universal compassion. More specifically, it is the realization that "all others are human beings who, just like oneself, aspire to happiness and shun suffering."[79] What he is describing is the spiritual consciousness that is expressed in the Golden Rule, the spirit of which he has articulated in talks on numerous occasions as the principle: "Help others, and if you cannot help them, leave them alone – do not harm them."[80] This is the core teaching of the Mahayana Buddhist tradition, asserts the Dalai Lama. In addition, he emphasizes that even though many people may benefit from a period of withdrawal from social life when first undertaking a spiritual practice, the goal of spiritual practice is not withdrawal from the world but active participation in society and service to others. In broad outline, natural spirituality as the Dalai Lama defines it appears to be quite similar to the religious/ethical humanism of Dewey and Fromm. It is one way to conceive the core meaning of being more.

The second half of *Beyond Religion* is devoted to presenting spiritual practices for overcoming the influence of destructive emotions and for cultivating universal compassion that can be used in a secular context. For the most part, the disciplines recommended are secularized versions of Tibetan Buddhist moral psychology and meditation practices. The Dalai Lama's approach in this regard is similar in a general way to that adopted by the larger mindfulness in education movement.

Beyond Religion recognizes that "it is vital that when educating our children's brains we do not neglect to educate their hearts, and a key element of educating their hearts has to be nurturing their compassionate nature." In this regard, the Dalai Lama argues that since religion no longer has the wide influence it once had and one can no longer assume that children learn spiritual and moral values at home, "it seems clear that the responsibility of schools in this area -spiritual and moral education – has greatly increased." "My hope and wish is that, one day, formal education will pay attention to what I call education of the heart…and that children will learn, as part of their school curriculum, the indispensability of inner values such as love, compassion, justice, and forgiveness." To be effective in addressing this challenge, however, "teaching by example is of paramount importance," states the Dalai Lama. Administrators and teachers must embody in their behavior the values that they are promoting. In 2005, The Dalai Lama Center for Peace and Education was formed in Vancouver, Canada, with the mission of promoting in schools a balance between educating the mind and educating the heart. The Center is also an advocate for social and emotional learning.[81]

In *The Righteous Mind: Why Good People Are Divided by Politics and Religion* (2012), Jonathan Haidt, the moral psychologist, provides an engaging account of psychological research that deepens our understanding of humanity's innate moral and spiritual capacities and the vital importance of relational spirituality. In addition, *The Righteous Mind* is a significant contribution to efforts to overcome the political and social polarization that afflicts the nation. "Politics and religion are both expressions of our underlying moral psychology," asserts Haidt, "and an understanding of that psychology can help to bring people together."[82]

Like Buber and Fromm, Haidt contends that human beings have a "dual nature," and like them, he has his own distinctive approach to exploring and explaining this complexity. He recognizes that much human behavior is self-centered and reflects an I-It or having character orientation. However, he rejects as unbalanced the widespread contemporary view that humanity is *Homo economicus*, a creature born selfish and competitive and motivated exclusively by self-interest even when cooperating with others, an outlook that reinforces self-centeredness and can promote mistrust of and hostility toward others. His experimental psychological research coupled with the study of Darwinian evolutionary theory, psychological anthropology, and the work of the sociologist, Emile Durkheim, leads him to the conclusion that human beings are *Homo duplex.*

> We, humans, have a dual nature – we are selfish primates who long to be part of something larger and nobler than ourselves. We are 90% chimp and 10% bee... We are not always selfish hypocrites. We also have the ability, under special circumstances, to shut down our petty selves and become like cells in a larger body, or like bees in a hive, working for the good of the group. These experiences are often among the most cherished of our lives.

Haidt argues that what enables people to shut down the selfish primate in their nature is the capacity to construct shared moral values and cooperate in support of common goals. It is morality that has made human civilization possible.[83]

Haidt's extensive psychological research provides convincing empirical evidence that the source of morality in human beings is a set of evolved, inborn moral emotions and intuitions, which he often describes as "gut feelings." His research leads him to reject the rationalism of the influential child psychologists, Jean Piaget and Lawrence Kohlberg, who contend that children, using reason, self-construct their moral values and principles. "Moral intuitions arise automatically, and almost instantaneously, long before reasoning has a chance to get started," explains Haidt. The new science reveals that this process begins very early in a child's development. As the mind matures, reason is used to defend and justify our moral intuitions and sometimes can influence them, but reason is not the foundation of morality. In this regard, the eighteenth-century Scottish philosopher, David Hume, got it right, asserts Haidt. "Intuitions come first, strategic reasoning second" is the first principle of his Moral Foundations Theory.[84]

Haidt uses Darwinian moral psychology to explain the origin of these moral intuitions. He contends that humanity's dual nature is the product of Darwinian natural selection operating simultaneously at both the individual and group level. For thousands of years, individuals have competed within groups, and people today are the descendants of the self-centered primates who excelled in that competition. Groups also competed with other groups, and Haidt reasons, as did Darwin, that the groups who were most successful in cooperating in support of shared values and common goals triumphed over groups dominated by uncooperative individuals. The human genome has evolved under the impact of cultural innovations related to morality ("gene-culture coevolution") as well as with the operation of natural selection at the individual level. In short, moral instincts and emotions are group-level adaptations and are part of the genetic makeup that forms human nature. People are "intrinsically moral" and "prewired" to be empathetic and to construct shared values and cooperate. However, skeptical about the human potential for universal compassion, Haidt contends that the altruism inspired by our genetic inheritance is for the most part group related. "We are not saints, but we are sometimes good team players."[85]

Haidt notes that in different cultures one encounters different moral matrices that reflect different views of the self and of how to balance the needs of the individual and the needs of groups and institutions. There are some universal principles like compassion, prevention of harm, fairness, and justice, but the emphasis on and understanding of these principles may vary, and across cultures, there are also some very real differences in the values and virtues governing everyday life. Searching for an understanding of this diverse moral landscape, his extensive psychological research conducted over a number of years in different cultures identifies six fundamental "moral foundations" at work in human nature. Each foundation is a "psychological mechanism" that involves a kind of perception and cognition (distinct from reason and like taste) and each awakens certain distinctive intuitions and emotions inspiring moral concerns and virtues. What his research leads him to propose regarding the wellsprings of morality is more complicated than theories that focus primarily on care, compassion, and avoidance of harm. Haidt's six evolved, universal moral foundations are: Care\harm; Liberty\oppression; Fairness\cheating; Loyalty\betrayal; Authority\subversion; and Sanctity\degradation. He emphasizes that a child's inherited moral instincts are flexible and are modified by the cultural environment and a person's education and experience. As a result, people end up embracing a variety of moral matrices, but they all reflect the influence of some or all of the six moral foundations. Haidt believes that morality is essential to building a better world and that his account of morality is true descriptively, but he avoids trying to argue that any particular moral matrix is the one true and valid morality for every society and for all time.[86]

The Righteous Mind explains that a major source of the political polarization in America is the differences in the moral matrices that govern liberal and conservative thinking. Morality "binds and blinds," states Haidt. His argument in this regard is complex. In brief, he asserts that the liberal moral matrix is "a three-foundation morality" focused on care, liberty, and fairness with a special emphasis on social reform guided by compassion for victims of oppression. Liberals view the individual as the basic unit of society and tend to be ambivalent about the values of loyalty, authority, and sanctity. The weakness of liberalism, argues Haidt, is that its advocates in their zeal for reform often make too many changes too fast and end up weakening institutions and the moral capital of society. He contends that the conservative moral matrix reflects the influence of all six moral foundations, which many social conservatives value equally. They tend to be supportive of a traditional socio-centric as distinct from an individualistic moral outlook. They view the self as interdependent and the family as the basic unit of society and are especially concerned to defend traditions and preserve institutions that protect and sustain moral communities. The weakness in the approach of conservatives is that in their concern to preserve order and stability they often fail to promote the institutional reforms needed to protect and support the oppressed and prevent the corruption and injustice perpetrated by the powerful.[87]

Haidt confesses that he was formerly a self-righteous liberal Democrat, who viewed conservatives as the enemy of the common good, and he could not understand what led people to vote for Republicans. What he learned as a psychologist caused a radical transformation in his thinking. He was led to understand that having a six-foundation morality that includes loyalty, authority, and sanctity actually gives conservatives an advantage in their political messaging, especially among rural and working-class voters. "I began to think about liberal and conservative policies as manifestations of deeply conflicting but equally heartfelt visions of the good society." Moreover, he came to believe that America needs the moral wisdom of both liberals and conservatives. He found it liberating "to be released from partisan anger." "It felt like a kind of awakening."[88]

As a humanist and a scientist, Haidt is primarily interested in the origin and function of morality, but his moral psychology includes a discussion of religion and what is best described as the spiritual dimension of experience. It is a mistake, he believes, to dismiss religion as just a matter of superstitious beliefs regarding supernatural agents as some atheists do. Religion, he suggests, is "an evolutionary adaptation for binding groups together and helping them create communities with a shared morality." He notes that "the psychology of the sacred," which involves endowing the core ideals of a group with infinite value, helps support and solidify commitment to moral communities. He also observes that the sacralizing of core values occur in the secular world and political sphere as well as within institutional religions. The binding of individuals into moral communities with a sacred center, which Haidt calls "hiving," opens people up to transformative spiritual experiences. When an individual transcends self-interest and embraces the ideals and values of a group, it can awaken a deep sense of connection and belonging, a sense of being "part of a whole," which, he states, is the source of "our greatest joy." Further, the feeling of being part of a whole can generate intuitions of an underlying oneness and of being part of the universe. Haidt notes that in addition to a merger in a moral community, such ecstatic intuitions and emotions can be stimulated in a variety of ways, such as in and through experiences of awe in nature, the practice of meditation, singing in a chorus, military drilling, and marching, etc. Supporting a natural and relational spirituality, Haidt concludes: "Happiness comes from between. It comes from getting the right relationship between yourself and others, yourself and your work, and yourself and something greater than yourself."[89]

"If the hive hypothesis is true," reasons Haidt, "then it has enormous implications for how we should design organizations, study religion, and search for meaning and joy in our lives." A stable, flourishing democracy with happy people is a nation full of hives with transformational leaders who understand the psychology of Homo duplex and know how to create strong organizations with healthy moral foundations that provide people with a deep sense of connection, belonging, meaning, and purpose.[90] Haidt's moral psychology affirms the existence of widely shared fundamental moral values such as care, prevention of harm, compassion, fairness, and justice. He also recognizes that there are at work in human nature other important dimensions of moral concern, and his research illuminates the genetic and social origins of much cultural diversity. In this regard, *The Righteous Mind* can help to promote the essential democratic virtue of tolerance and respect for cultural diversity and make American politics more civil.

Regarding the implications of his vision for Pre-K-12 education, schools should be hives, institutions with transformational leaders who have the ability to bind young people together in inspiring moral communities that nurture the unique intellectual and spiritual potential of each student and promote what Dewey called shared experience in the midst of America's diversity. In a recent essay on how social media platforms like Facebook, Instagram, and Twitter have become major forces contributing to the polarization, fragmentation, and mental health crisis in America, Haidt emphasizes the urgent need to better prepare the next generation to deal with the corrosive impact of social media and to rebuild "trust and friendship across the political divide."[91]

7

Awakened Awareness and America's Schools

Lisa Miller's most recent book, *The Awakened Brain*, is both an account of her own spiritual odyssey and the story of her quest as a research scientist in the fields of psychology, epidemiology, and neuroscience for an understanding of natural spirituality and its significance for human health and wellbeing. Miller's personal spiritual life has provided her with the kinds of direct, immediate experiences that over the centuries have led many people in all cultures to take seriously, treasure, and promote spiritual values and ideals. However, as a trained clinical psychologist and psychotherapist with new methods of scientific research available, Miller is not content to promote and theorize about spirituality simply based on her personal spiritual experiences and the related testimony of others, important as that is. The problem she discovered is that in spite of the insights of psychologists like William James and psychotherapists such as Viktor Frankl and Erich Fromm, the reigning theory embraced by practitioners of psychoanalysis and psychotherapy does not take spirituality and religion seriously as a source of mental health and wellbeing. It is easy for psychologists and therapists to dismiss religion as an illusion and an interest in spirituality as a crutch or defense mechanism. Moreover, in her observation, the methods being used to treat depression and other forms of mental suffering, which include the wide use of medications as well as psychotherapy, are not working in many cases. Her interactions with patients as well as her own spiritual experience convinced her that the dominant psychological paradigm is missing something fundamental about mental health and spirituality.[92]

With a primary focus on "whether or not spirituality plays a role in preventing or protecting against depression," Miller set out to find hard scientific evidence that would drive a radical change in the dominant attitude toward and understanding of spirituality, demonstrating that in fact, spirituality plays a central role in protecting against depression. Beginning in 1995, she began looking for "a concrete physiological function of spirituality in our health and development." To this end, she began using new complex methods of statistical modeling for analyzing large collections of data relevant to how spirituality correlates with the risk for depression. She also employed the new technologies being developed by neuroscience, such as magnetic resonance imagining (MRI), to study the impact of spirituality on the neural structure of the brain. Her findings, which are startling, deepen our understanding of human nature and mental health and healing.[93]

Before considering some of Miller's most important findings, some clarification regarding what she means by spirituality is in order. As is the case with the term religion, there is no consensus among scholars as to just how to define spirituality, and Miller does not attempt to provide a short definition. She recognizes that there are a great variety of experiences that can be categorized as spiritual in nature, and in her book, she describes many of them. Much of what she describes regarding the spiritual dimension of experience is consistent with the views of other thinkers considered in this essay. She contends that spirituality involves a distinctive "way of being in the world" and that there are certain universal aspects of spirituality. For example, it takes a person "beyond a one-track intellectual way of knowing the world and into a felt awareness of life." Spirituality opens a person up to the experiential insights and knowing that can come through intuition, feeling, emotion, and gut reactions, which can provide illumination and guidance in the midst of life's challenges and suffering. "An awakened heart is the seat of...spiritual perception," states Miller.[94]

Many spiritual experiences involve transcending the confines of the ego and a sense of separateness and awakening a feeling of being part of something greater than the self. In deep spiritual experiences, there is a sense of relationship, or union, with a higher power, God, the life force, nature, or the universe. Such experiences generate "a feeling of oneness and connection" and "a sense of transcendent unity." Of special importance, such experiences can give people a deep faith or trust in the meaning and value of life in spite of all that might lead them to despair. In this regard, Miller writes about "the foundational, felt awareness that we are loved and held and part of it all" -- "that life itself holds us in a loving embrace." In addition, she identifies empathy, love of others, compassion, altruism, and adherence to a moral code as universal aspects of spiritual life.[95] The moral life can be considered part of spiritual life insofar as moral concern is inspired from within by empathy, care, and compassion as opposed to being motivated by unthinking social conformity or fear of and obedience to external authorities.

What Miller discovered using an MRI scanner is especially revealing. It shows that the neural brain structure of people with stable and high spirituality is much stronger and healthier than the brain structure of people with low spirituality. In addition, "the high-spiritual brain was thicker and stronger in *exactly the same regions* that weaken and wither in depressed brains." Miller also used functional magnetic resonance imaging (fMRI) to map the neural correlates of spiritual experiences, linking the different aspects of spiritual experiences with specific regions of the brain. "We'd found the neural docking station of love, unity, and guidance," she writes.[96]

Regarding the degree to which a person's spirituality is determined by an inborn capacity or is the product of socialization, Miller discovered an answer in the research on spirituality in Kenneth Kendler's twin studies. "A person's degree of spirituality" and "capacity to experience the sacred and transcendent" is one-third inherited, inscribed in our genetic code, and two-thirds the result of our social environment. Kendler's research and her MRI studies provide convincing empirical evidence that "just as we are cognitive, physical, and emotional beings, we are spiritual beings." "Spirituality is an innate foundational way of being ...for which we are hard-wired," states Miller. It is not just a matter of religious beliefs a person chooses to adopt. It is "a genetic capacity within us" for a fundamental dimension of experience. As with all human abilities, the strength of a person's capacity for spiritual development varies from individual to individual, and the development of this inborn spiritual capacity is profoundly influenced by "how we are raised, the company we keep, the things we do to build the muscle."[97]

Some further examples of Miller's findings are the following. Adolescents with a strong personal spiritual life are 35 to 75 percent less likely than others to experience clinical depression and are 40 to 80 percent less likely to develop substance dependence or abuse. "No other mental health intervention, clinical or pharmacological, for...adolescents has anything close to these prevention rates," asserts Miller. In addition, she found that "those who had strong spirituality by age twenty-six were 75 percent protected against a recurrence of major depression for the next ten years." Recognizing that "the same piece of our genetic wiring carried both the risk for depression and the capacity to be spiritually aware," Miller came to realize that "the condition we pathologize and diagnose as depression is sometimes actually spiritual hunger – a normal genetically derived part of human development that it is unhealthy to muffle and deny." What if the elevated rates of depression and addiction among teens, she asks, are "because young people are struggling to form spiritually" and we are not supporting them?[98]

A research project on universal dimensions of spirituality conducted by Miller revealed that people committed to the love of neighbor and altruism have "enhanced cortical thickness across the spiritual network of the brain... providing structural protection against depression" and indicating "a robust protective benefit of **relational spirituality**, a personal spirituality that emphasizes both our commitment to other humans and our awareness of a transcendent or higher power." Miller adds: "If you take Prozac to treat depression, and then stop taking the medication, you could potentially be depressed again in a matter of weeks. But our study suggested that daily, lived altruism may be curative." Why? "Maybe because it restores us to ourselves – to our optimum functioning, and also to an accurate perception of the nature of life."[99]

Summarizing her findings regarding the awakened brain, Miller writes:

> Each of us is endowed with a natural capacity to perceive a greater reality and consciously connect to the life force that moves in, through, and around us...The awakened brain includes a set of innate perceptual capacities that exist in every person through which we experience love and connection, unity, and a sense of guidance. And when we engage these perceptual capacities...our brains become structurally healthier and better connected, and we access unsurpassed psychological benefits: less depression, anxiety, and substance abuse; and more positive psychological traits such as grit, resilience, optimism, tenacity, and creativity...Beyond belief, beyond a cognitive story, we tell ourselves, the awakened brain is the inner lens through which we access the truest and most expansive reality: that all of life is sacred, that we never walk alone. Our brains are wired to perceive and receive that which uplifts, illuminates, and heals.

Miller's research is carrying forward in innovative ways the scientific exploration of spiritual experience that was pioneered by William James over a century ago, confirming and deepening his insights into the vital importance of spirituality for human development and wellbeing. It is also noteworthy that Miller's thinking regarding natural spirituality is consistent in many respects with John Dewey's naturalistic theory of the religious (spiritual) dimension of experience. Dewey, as well as James, would enthusiastically support her search for a scientific understanding of spirituality and its function.

Using the new science to construct a distinctive variation on a theme encountered in the spiritual writings of thinkers like Buber, Fromm, and Haidt, Miller makes the case that "we all have two modes of awareness available to us at all times: achieving awareness and awakened awareness." "Achieving awareness," she writes, "is the perception that our purpose is to organize and control our lives." Its major concern is: *How can I get and keep what I want?*" It generates the character orientation that Buber identified with I-It interactions and that Fromm described as focused on having more and the tendency to reduce every person and thing to its utilitarian value. The function of the achieving brain is necessary for survival and has many practical benefits. However, when it becomes dominant, "achieving awareness overrides and changes the structure of our brains, carving pathways of depression, anxiety, stress and craving" that easily lead to addiction and destructive patterns of behavior. The path to healing, wholeness, and well-being is awakened awareness and being more, leading to a sense of the sacredness of all life, caring, compassion, shared experience, and I-Thou relationships. In a healthy brain, achieving and awakened awareness are integrated. "We make our best decisions," writes Miller, "when we integrate our heads, hearts, and life's guidance."[100]

Regarding the larger significance of the awakened brain, Miller states:

> The awakened brain…gives us a new paradigm for being, leading, and relating that can help us act with greater clarity and capability as we face humanity's greatest challenges…I've come to see the problems we have in leadership, education, social justice, the environment, and mental health as different emanations of the same problem: unawakened awareness.

Miller adds: "Each one of us has the ability to fully develop our innate capacity to live through an awareness of love, interconnection, and appreciation of life's unfolding...But we have to choose to engage it. It's a muscle we have to learn to strengthen or let atrophy." What gives her hope is that both the individual and society at large benefit when people chose spiritual development. "Our individual health and flourishing depend on our choice to awaken. So do the health and flourishing of our schools, workplaces, governments – and the planet...Everyone gains when we open our hearts to others and to all life." In the concluding chapters of The Awakened Brain, Miller offers practical guidance on how to nurture awakened awareness.[101] By promoting an understanding of natural spirituality, she helps clarify the meaning and importance of spiritual democracy for all institutions and American society at large. Awakened awareness, being more, relational spirituality, compassion, love, and altruism are the driving forces at work in spiritual democracy.

Miller's research has led her to become a nationally recognized advocate for the education of the whole child and the conviction that supporting the development of the inborn spiritual and moral capacities of young people and integrating the achieving brain and the awakened brain should be a fundamental goal of education in America. Tragically many young people lose touch with their heart and spiritual core as the years pass, and their spiritual life is shut down and goes dormant. This can happen if during the school years their innate spiritual feelings, instincts, perceptions, intuitions, yearnings, aspirations, doubts, and questions are dismissed and neglected and their spiritual growth is not actively supported and nurtured by parents, teachers, religious leaders, and the larger community. This is today the all too common experience of growing numbers of young people. It is a tragedy for the individual and society and the future of humanity and life on Earth. The fault is often with education in the home and the school as well as with the cultural environment in the larger society.

Many educators concerned with the education of the whole child have tended to focus primarily on the curriculum and on teaching in the sense of sharing information and imparting skills. However, after completing a two-year study of 21 outstanding independent and public schools with a commitment to spirituality in education, some religious and some secular, Professor Miller was led to conclude that carefully designing and building a school culture and pervasive ethos supportive of whole child development and spiritual awareness is the most effective strategy. The social environment in which children live at home and in school is the most powerful force promoting their socialization and shaping their values, attitudes, dispositions, desires, and beliefs. Culture impacts a child's deep inner core, the heart, the center of the whole child, for good or ill, in a way that much teaching (and preaching) does not. In addition, an emphasis on school culture, what today is often called school climate, recognizes that with regard to spirituality the most crucial need is to support and nurture the development of a child's inborn spiritual and moral capacities and their natural instincts, feelings, intuitions, and aspirations as distinct from teaching the child about spirituality. What is taught as well as how it is taught is, of course, also very important. Opportunities to participate in the creative and performing arts can engage a young person's whole being. Courses in literature, poetry, history, philosophy, religion, and ethics, and the story of the universe as science is coming to understand it, are among the many that can contribute to a young person's spiritual growth as well as their intellectual development, especially when the teacher is spiritually awake and alive.

Lisa Miller's research involving the 21 leadership schools led to the identification of 11 Drivers of a Transformative School Culture, which can help schools design and reconstruct their culture. The most critical Driver was found to be "Building student-teacher relationships grounded in connection and love." The most effective way to awaken moral insight and awaken a spiritual way of being in young people is to provide them with the direct experience of interacting with a caring, kind, and responsible parent, teacher, or mentor. A young person's capacity to love grows with the experience of being loved. I-thou relationships can make all the difference. Among the other 11 Drivers are the following:

- Seeing, knowing, and valuing every member of the school community.
- Vertically integrating a living and meaningful mission
- Promoting community identity and belonging among diverse staff and students through ritual and celebration
- Committing to drawing out the deep spirit and creative expression of every child.
- Facilitating opportunities to form deep, lived relationships with nature and all life.[102]

Each school has to find its own unique way to build a spiritually supportive school culture that harmonizes with its distinctive history, traditions, and local situation. This involves developing its own language for advancing the project. In this regard, some schools may choose to talk explicitly about promoting spirituality. Some may use the language of religion. Others may choose not to focus attention on the word spirituality. A school can support spiritual values and nurture natural spirituality and spiritual democracy without necessarily talking about spirituality if that presents a problem. Miller is now in the process of launching at Teachers College the Awakened Schools Institute, which is sharing the findings of the new science with schools and training principals and teachers as they endeavor to build spiritually supportive schools. The times call for imaginative thinking and creative innovations as schools strive to meet this challenge.

In this connection, it is useful to summarize the understanding in this essay regarding what is meant by spirituality when one is promoting spirituality in America's public and independent PreK-12 schools. Spirituality in this context means caring in age-appropriate ways for the heart and spirit of young people as well as their mind and body. It is to be identified with natural spirituality and the development of a young person's inborn spiritual and moral capacities leading to awakened awareness. It is concerned to support and nurture spiritual democracy, a relational spirituality associated with the universal aspirations and values set forth in the nation's founding documents, and with respect and care for the greater community of life.

The heart is the inner core of a person's being, the deep center of the feeling, thinking, willing, and acting human being. The spirit is also to be identified with the deep inner core. The heart is a spiritual faculty, and the activity of the spirit, its feelings, intuitions, and aspirations, is the heart at work. It is the spirit that integrates heart and head. The spirit of an individual or a people is expressed in their way of being, which is formed by the attitudes, values, desires, and beliefs that motivate them and guide how they truly think and actually behave. A person's way of being determines the quality of the individual's relationships with the self, other persons, other cultures, the greater community of life, and the mystery of being. A heart that is in the grip of fear, hatred, and despair and is closed will prevent the healthy growth of the spirit. A heart that is possessed by trust and faith in the meaning and value of life and is open will inspire a wholehearted yes to life and positive spiritual growth. When we think about the spirit of a young person it includes the recognition that every child is a unique individual with distinctive abilities and qualities who brings into the world special gifts. Spirituality in education involves creating the conditions that make possible the blossoming and growth of a young person's spirit. The process cannot be forced. The growth of a young person's spirit has its own times and seasons. As in a garden, if the right conditions are prepared, beautiful things can happen.

When basic needs have been met, spiritual growth, the path to meaning, fulfillment, and joy, comes in and through being more as distinct from having more. Being more involves releasing "the energy hiding in our hearts" – the wonder and awe, the appreciation of beauty, the moral intuitions, the sense of the sacred, the yearning for wholeness and self-expression, the quest for connection and loving relationships, the desire to be part of something greater than the self. It involves opening our hearts and minds to the world, cultivating our inborn capacities for awakened awareness, and ever-expanding and deepening our consciousness. It is all about integrating head and heart, science and faith, intelligence and compassion, freedom and responsibility, justice and mercy, and realizing our unique potential as human beings. Happiness in the deeper sense is not found by directly seeking it. It comes as a gift of grace. It is a by-product of growing as a whole person, being more, and right relationship.

Schools that are committed to supporting spiritual democracy and natural spirituality create communities where each and every child is welcomed as a young person with inherent dignity full of unique potential and promise, whose birthright is freedom and who is worthy of society's protection and care. They are communities where students in all their diversity and uniqueness feel respected, understood, and loved and where they can develop a deep sense of self-worth, belonging, meaning, and purpose. They are communities that nurture the process of being more with the goal of preparing young people to live with an open heart that sees the light enabling them to forge meaningful relationships, learn from shared experience, serve society as responsible democratic citizens, and pursue never-ending growth as a whole person.

Caring for children is a demanding task, but most young children are in touch with their inner spiritual being. The consciousness reflected in the myth of the Garden of Eden is to some degree still with them. Their hearts tend to be open. They spontaneously greet the world with wonder and yearn to grow and learn. They seek avenues for self-expression. They naturally feel empathy in relation to others and want to belong and be part of something greater than the self. They search for meaning and purpose and transcendence and joy. However, with the awakening of the rational intellect, the emergence of self-consciousness, and the formation of the ego, the situation of young people becomes increasingly complex intellectually and spiritually. Feelings of separation and estrangement during adolescence become forces to contend with. The young person must learn that the lost unity cannot be found by regressing and going back but can only be recovered by further expanding their consciousness and developing their unique individuality. Their spiritual development involves discovering the truth in Rabbi Hillel's three questions: "If I am not for myself, who will be? And if I am only for myself, what am I? If not now, when?" This is where spirituality intersects with the ethics of democracy.

Awakening and supporting in young people their innate spiritual capacity for inner freedom is especially important. In contrast with totalitarian societies, which do not trust that the mass of people is capable of managing freedom, democratic societies are built on the faith that if the right conditions are created, human beings can handle freedom and that becoming free is necessary for the full realization of the human potential. In the democratic tradition, the unique dignity of the human being is commonly associated with the possession of reason and a moral conscience (innate moral intuitions) and with the capacity for independence of thought and freedom of choice. This includes the development of the inner freedom to choose what kind of person one wants to become and be. As individuals, we have only very limited control over how other people behave and over what happens in the larger world around us. However, we do have the ability to determine what attitude we will adopt in response to whatever circumstances, good or bad, life thrusts us. We can choose, for example, to manage the destructive emotions like anger and hatred that cause harmful behavior and strive to keep our hearts open and remain faithful to our ideals in difficult situations, even in the face of unfairness, oppression, and suffering.

The wisdom, strength, and courage to exercise this inner freedom in positive ways comes from our deep inner core and grows in and through the spiritual process of being more. It requires cultivating self-knowledge, self-discipline, and social awareness together with one's innate capacity for moral responsibility and compassion. The Stoic philosophers called it the last freedom because it is a freedom no one can take away. It is the deepest source of human dignity. It can, however, go undeveloped, and people can allow themselves to be guided by delusion, self-centeredness, an I-It mindset, the crowd, fear, craving, and hatred. The strength and health of a free society depend on individual citizens cultivating their capacity for this inner freedom and being prepared to exercise it in defense of democratic ideals and ecological values when they are threatened.

8

Conclusion:
A Transformative
National Movement

America is in the midst of a complex social crisis that reflects a profound loss of shared spiritual and moral values. What is needed is a renewal of the American democratic faith and spirit, and the schools have a critical contribution to make. As a nation dedicated to freedom, equality, unalienable rights, the rule of law, justice, and the common good, America requires a moral and spiritual foundation that supports and inspires the caring, trust, compassion, love, and cooperation essential to the building of a better world that works for all and protects Earth's ecological integrity. This essay has identified these democratic ideals and ethical values and their implementation in everyday life with spiritual democracy, a relational spirituality. It also argues that spiritual democracy can be supported by the cultivation of what some psychologists call natural spirituality and identify with the healthy growth and development of a person's inner being or spirit and way of life.

The new science of psychology and spirituality is clarifying the concept of natural spirituality, providing empirical evidence that human beings are by nature social, moral, and spiritual beings. We are born with innate capacities for a felt awareness of the meaning, value, and sacredness of life and for empathy, compassion, cooperation, and a sense of fairness and justice. It is also the case that these inborn capacities must be actively supported and nurtured or they can be lost. The new science has demonstrated that cultivating these capacities and values is essential for the health and thriving of individuals as well as the well-being of society. This is the underlying issue that must be addressed if, for example, America is to succeed in ending its tragic history of racism and is to find common ground and work out intelligent, ethically responsible policy resolutions that free future generations from fighting interminable, debilitating culture wars.

The human situation, however, is complex. The struggle for survival in the natural world is real, and in and through the process of evolution human beings have developed extraordinary capacities and powers for analyzing, controlling, dominating, and using the world around them. Modern science and technology are, for example, the products of these powers. Caring, compassion, and cooperation on the one hand, and having, controlling, and using, on the other hand, are both essential. This situation confronts humanity with a great spiritual challenge that becomes ever more urgent as humanity's powers of control, creation, and destruction grow. Human beings must choose and decide which of two modes of existence, two basic attitudes or character orientations, they will adopt as the guiding way of being in their lives and in the societies they build. These two modes have been described in various ways using different conceptual frameworks, and this essay has cited some examples, including head and heart; me and we; I-It and I-Thou; centering on what we want from life and on what life expects from us; having more and being more; achieving awareness and awakened awareness.

The critical issue regarding a head-centered or I-It approach in relation to the world is that this orientation sees self and world as separated and reduces everything to its utilitarian value, to a means only. It views the world through the lens of the ego and scientific materialism. Other persons and living beings are perceived as things to be analyzed, possessed, and used. If this awareness is the only or overwhelmingly dominant awareness a people have, they live in a constantly changing world made up of things with no intrinsic value. In such a world, one can try to find meaning, purpose, and happiness by pursuing wealth, power, fame, and pleasure, but death, if not sickness and misfortune, will take these things from you. It is a world with no ultimate meaning and value that supports selfishness, tribalism, and endless competition and conflict. When honestly faced it can only generate desperation, depression, and despair. Moreover, it is people with an unchecked I-It mindset and orientation who over the centuries have led human beings to kill, subjugate, dominate, enslave, exploit, and exclude other peoples, causing crimes against humanity and terrible suffering. Vladimir Putin's horrifying war against Ukraine is a prime example of this mindset at work. The same character orientation leads to the ruthless exploitation of the larger natural world, devastating the greater community of life and undermining the ecological health of the planet.

What spiritual teachers have long known and what psychologists like Lisa Miller have been able to support with scientific research is that human beings have an additional inborn way of perceiving reality and relating to life. This power of awakened awareness, which involves feelings, mystical intuitions, gut reactions, perceptions, longings, and aspirations that arise within and grip the heart, includes a yearning to transcend a self-centered, I-It worldview. Awakened awareness senses an underlying oneness and the interdependence of all things and responds to the gift of life and the mystery of being with wonder, reverence, and gratitude. It respects the inherent and equal dignity in other persons and the intrinsic value of all life forms. It is open to spiritual guidance. It understands the truth in the moral imperative to help others and avoid harming them, to cooperate in building community, and to strive for justice and peace. It perceives that the protection of the environment is an urgent moral issue. Awakened awareness inspires relations with the world in all its diversity guided by compassion, love, tolerance, repentance, and forgiveness integrated with the practical understanding that knowledge of the It world can provide. In and through this way of being, a person can be possessed and sustained by a deep sense of belonging to the universe and an abiding trust that there is a path to authentic freedom and fulfillment and that our lives have profound, enduring meaning and value.

This natural spirituality and awakened awareness are what makes progress toward the ideals envisioned with the creation of American democracy a real possibility. It is the wisdom and inspiration that is spiritual democracy. Young people are at formative stages in their development when their inner spirit is searching for a way of being that will lead to ongoing growth, connection, wholeness, and fulfillment. Especially since our way of being determines how we will take up and pursue our responsibilities as democratic citizens, given all we now know about human nature and natural spirituality, why would America not want to support the natural spirituality of its youth as a fundamental dimension of their education?

It is noteworthy that Lisa Miller's science has attracted the attention of the US Army at the highest levels in the Pentagon. Like much of American society, the military is contending with a mental health crisis and serious behavioral problems, especially among younger service members. For example, the Army is losing more soldiers to suicide than combat and is facing persistent problems with sexual assault and right-wing extremism. Impressed by Miller's research findings regarding spirituality and its protective benefits, the Army has engaged her as a consultant and adviser on spiritual preparedness. She has been sent to Army bases across the country and overseas to educate commanders, chaplains, and non-commissioned officers regarding the new science of spirituality and how to support the spiritual growth and awareness of service members.

Another significant development is the growing interest among corporate leaders in spiritual development as essential for effective leadership and decision-making in business. Bob Chapman, the CEO of Barry-Wehmiller, has put the idea into practice and in the process has demonstrated that when done well it can benefit a business, its employees, their families, and the larger society in fundamental ways. Chapman's book, *Everybody Matters: The Extraordinary Power of Caring for Your People Like Family*, provides a compelling account of the transformation of consciousness and spiritual awakening he underwent as a corporate leader causing him to abandon the I-It attitude in relation to his company's employees (treating them as objects, functions, resources only) that he had learned in business school. Inspired by deepening awakened awareness, he transformed his company's corporate culture guided by the principle that leadership is first and foremost about caring for people and promoting their growth and fulfillment, recognizing that every human being deserves to be treated with dignity and respect.[103] His story is a prime example of what spiritual democracy and natural spirituality mean when applied in the business world and other institutions. It is what thinkers like Dewey, Buber, and Fromm imagined could happen when they called for an integration of spiritual life and everyday life.

What the generals at the Pentagon are doing inspired by Lisa Miller's science and understanding of natural spirituality and what Bob Chapman, inspired by awakened awareness, is doing at Barry-Wehmiller, is the kind of transformative action that federal and state educational leaders and school principals and teachers should be undertaking in the schools. Young people urgently need the support, and America's institutions in all spheres require well-prepared, mentally strong and healthy, spiritually aware citizens among whom there are able future leaders. The good news is that when all the path-breaking research and programs in support of holistic education, mindfulness, SEL, civic education, awakened awareness, and other related initiatives are taken into consideration, it becomes evident that over the last three decades a new transformative national movement has emerged in support of education for the whole child, and within this movement, there is growing support for spirituality in education. It is a diverse movement without any centralized organizational structure driven by multiple organizations each with its own special vision and focus. There are different dimensions to the challenge and the diversity of approaches has many benefits. There is much yet to be discovered and to learn. However, a substantial literature on the new science and effective strategies and techniques has already been created. Many schools are committed to the task, and thousands of teachers are being trained. There is also cross-fertilization of ideas and some overlap and collaboration between, for example, holistic education and spirituality in education, the mindfulness movement and SEL, and civic education and SEL. The National Council on Spirituality in Education, which is managed by the Collaborative for Spirituality in Education, periodically brings representatives from multiple organizations and groups together around an explicit focus on spirituality in education, which is the core of the challenge facing educators looking to the future.

These developments merit wide support from civil society, business, and government. The best way to expand the work of this movement in the public schools is to make clear that in addition to providing urgently needed support for America's young people what is at stake is the rebuilding of the nation's moral and spiritual foundations and renewing American democracy. The schools can do this without promoting or opposing religion by supporting spiritual democracy, natural spirituality, and awakened awareness. Commitment to these values can create a greater sense of common purpose and unity in the midst of diversity among the many groups involved, and build increased public support for the movement and for teachers and schools in general. The integration of holistic education, mindfulness, SEL, and spirituality in education with the civic and history education movements is especially important. The new American history should give young people a realistic understanding of human nature and address the moral failures, oppression, and injustice that are tragically part of the nation's history. However, the deeper meaning of American history is found in a profoundly positive story. It is the story of an extraordinary, ongoing struggle against the darkness and for the light - for freedom, equality, justice, ecological integrity, and the common good – led by courageous men and women from all races, religions, and ethnic backgrounds. When told with a passion for the ideals and values at the heart of the story, the nation's history can awaken in each generation of young people pride in their national identity and help to inspire the faith, hope, caring, and determination they need to carry on the work of building America to be what it should become.

America is at a critical crossroads. A friendly visitor from outer space observing the state of human consciousness and behavior in the US and around the world today would likely conclude that human beings may not have the faith, wisdom, and courage to manage freedom and self-government. Support for democracy has been declining worldwide in recent decades, and democracy in America is still a social and political experiment. Whether a very diverse people from around the world can come together in freedom and cooperatively build a dynamic, creative society that recognizes the equal dignity of every person and promotes justice, sustainable development, peace, and the welfare of all, including future generations, is not yet a settled matter. It is a question as to whether human spiritual and moral consciousness can evolve fast enough to keep up with and ahead of the development of science and technology and the human capacity to possess, control, exploit, and destroy. Will America make a commitment to support and nurture the spiritual and moral capacities of its young people, their hearts and spirits, as well as their minds? Will shared experience overcome estrangement? Will being more and I-Thou relationships supersede the dominance of having more and I-It ways of interacting? Will awakened awareness come to guide our achieving awareness? If Americans want successfully to carry forward the work of building a nation dedicated to freedom, equality, justice, and the common good in the twenty-first century, these are questions that they must face. Without the support of the schools for spiritual democracy, natural spirituality, and awakened awareness, it is difficult to imagine how freedom and constitutional democracy in America can be sustained and flourish and how America will be able to serve as an inspiring leader in global efforts to build a just, sustainable and peaceful world.

Endnotes

Chapter 1 – The Spiritual Dimension of the Growing Crisis

[1] Robert D. Putnam with Shaylyn Romney Garrett, *The Upswing: How America Came Together a Century Ago and How We Can Do It Again* (New York: Simon & Schuster, 2020), 10-13, 306.

[2] Commission on the Practice of Democractic Citizenship, "Our Common Purpose: Reinventing American Democracy For the 21st Century" (Cambridge, Mass.: American Academy of Arts & Sciences, 2020), 1-22, 57-64. The Commission co-chairs include Danielle Allen, Stephen Heintz, and Eric Liu.

[3] See www.earthcharter.org.

[4] As quoted in Robert Gipe, "Appalachia Is More Diverse Than You Think," New York Times OpEd, March 16, 2019, A25.

[5] Jonathon Haidt, *The Righteous Mind: Why Good People Are Divided by Politics and Religion* (New York: Vintage Books, 2012), 364.

[6] Parker J. Palmer, *Healing the Heart of Democracy: The Courage to Create a Politics Worthy of the Human Spirit* (San Francisco: Josey-Bass, 2011), 6, 10, 18.

Chapter 2 – Democracy as an Ethical Ideal and Way of Life

[7] For a further discussion of these issues, see Steven C. Rockefeller, "Renewing the American Democratic Faith," in *Democracy Unchained: How to Rebuild Government for the People*, ed. David W. Orr, et al (New York: The New Press, 2020), 107-121.

[8] Gordon S. Wood, "Constitutional Freedoms," book review of *The Crooked Path to Abolition: Abraham Lincoln and the Antislavery Constitution*, by James Oakes, New York Times Book Review, January 24, 2021, 10. Times Book Review, January 24, 2021, 10.

[9] Federalist Paper 45.

[10] As cited in Gordon S. Wood, *Power and Liberty: Constitutionalism in the American Revolution* (Oxford University Press, 2021), 119.

[11] For the full text of Langston Hughes beautiful and moving poem, see Langston Hughes, *The Collected Poems of Langston Hughes,* ed. Arnold Rampersad (New York, Knopf, 1994). See also, Philip Gorski, *American Covenant: A History of Civil Religion from the Puritans to the Present* (Princeton: Princeton University Press, 2017), 223.

[12] James Baldwin, *The Fire Next Time* (New York: Vintage International, 1963), 8-10, 47, 92-106. On Baldwin, see also Michelle Alexander, review of *Between the World and Me*, by Ta-Nehisi Coates, in New York Times Book Review, August 17, 2015, reprinted October 24, 2021, 46-47.

[13] Martin Luther King, Jr. as quoted in Philip Gorski, *American Covenant: A History of Civil Religion from the Puritans to the Present* (Princeton: Princeton University Press, 2017), 148-157.

[14] Amanda Gorman, *The Hill We Climb: An Inaugural Poem for the Country* (New York: Viking, 2021), 13, 29.

[15] Steven C. Rockefeller, *John Dewey: Religious Faith and Democratic Humanism* (New York: Columbia University Press), 154-158. The overview of Dewey's thought in this essay is based on research presented in this intellectual biography of Dewey, which focuses special attention on the religious (spiritual) dimension of his thought.

[16] Ibid., 150-151, 154-168. The theory of "the religious dimension of experience" that Dewey developed as a philosophical naturalist and humanist is set forth in A Common Faith (1934). See Rockefeller, *John Dewey*, Chapter 10, Religious Humanism.

[17] John Dewey, *Freedom and Culture*, in *John Dewey: The Later Works, 1925-1953*, ed. Jo Ann Boydston (Carbondale, Ill.: Southern Illinois University Press, 1987), vol. 13: 178. In Freedom and Culture, Dewey also states: "With the founders of American Democracy, the claims of democracy were inherently one with the demands of a just and equal morality…the task of those who retain belief in democracy is to revive and maintain in full vigor the original conviction of the intrinsic moral nature of democracy, now stated in ways congruous with present conditions of culture. We have advanced far enough to say that democracy is a way of life. We have yet to realize that it is a way of personal life

and one which provides a moral standard for personal conduct." John Dewey: The Later Works, vol. 13: 154-155.

[18] "Creative Democracy – The Task Before Us," in *John Dewey: The Later Works,* vol.14: 225-228.

[19] Rockefeller, *John Dewey,* 234-246, 476-484. John Dewey, Liberalism and Social Action, in John Dewey: The Later Works, vol. 11: 41.

[20] Rockefeller, *John Dewey,* 236-246.

[21] Ibid., 197, 245-246.

[22] Ibid., 495-512. As a mature thinker, Dewey identified his philosophical outlook as a form of humanism and naturalism. Being a humanist meant to Dewey a focus on the problems of people and a belief that human beings have the innate capacities to make progress in building cooperatively a better world. As a philosophical naturalist, he held that there is one world, the world of nature, of which human beings are an interdependent part. He abandoned the idea of the supernatural and belief in the God of biblical theism. However, as this essay notes, he continued to take seriously the religious dimension of experience, and he rejected a despairing atheism and pessimistic views of the human future.

Chapter 3 – Spiritual Democracy for the 21st Century

[23] The use of the word dignity to describe the inherent worth of the human person has a long history in Western thought. The contemporary emphasis on the term can be traced back to the humanistic spirit and fresh focus on "the dignity of man" in much philosophical and religious literature during the Renaissance and Reformation. See John Herman Randall, Jr., *The Making of the Modern Mind* (Houghton Mifflin Company, 1940), 111-115,122-123,137-150.

[24] Rockefeller, "Renewing the American Democratic Faith," 13-19, 22-24.

[25] Jonathan Haidt, the moral psychologist, explores these issues with illuminating insights in *The Righteous Mind.*

[26] Thomas Berry, "Our Way into the Future: A Communion

of Subjects," in *Evening Thoughts: Reflecting on Earth as a Sacred Community,* ed. Mary Evelyn Tucker (Berkeley, Calif.: Counterpoint Press, 2015), 17. See also Mary Evelyn Tucker, John Grim, and Andrew Angyal, *Thomas Berry: A Biography* (New York: Columbia University Press, 2019), 144, 204, 258-259.

[27] See Brian Swimme and Thomas Berry, *The Universe Story* (HarperSanFransico, 1992) and Brian Swimme and Mary Evelyn Tucker, Journey of the Universe (New Haven: Yale University Press, 2011). https//wwwjourneyoftheuniverse.org.

[28] I am indebted to Professor Tu Wei Ming, the Confucian philosopher, for sharing with me a diagram of spiritual and moral consciousness very similar to what is presented here in this essay.

Chapter 4 – Democracy, Education, and Spirituality

[29] Mark A. Chancey, "The Bible and American Public Schools," in *The Oxford Handbook of Religion and American Education*, ed. Michael D. Waggoner and Nathaniel C. Walker (Oxford, Oxford University Press, 2018), 271-279. Stephen Prothero, *Religious Literacy: What Every American Needs to Know – and Doesn't* (HarperCollins Publisher, 2008), 73-152.

[30] Rockefeller, *John Dewey,* 233-236, 246-269. On Dewey and the Progressive Education movement, see Lawrence A. Cremin, *The Transformation of the School: Progressivism in American Education, 1876-1957* (New York: Alfred Knopf, 1961).

[31] Warreen Lee Cohen and Brian Daniel Bresnihan, "Waldorf Education: Freeing the Human Being" and Michael Dorer, Tim Seldin, Robin Howe, and Jennie Caskey, "Holism in Montessori," in *International Handbook of Holistic Education,* ed. John P. Miller et al (New York: Routledge, 2019),153-169.

[32] Candy Gunther Brown, *Debating Yoga and Mindfulness in Public Schools: Reforming Secular Education or Reestablishing Religion?* (Chapel Hill: University of North Carolina Press, 2019), 19-38.

[33] John P. Miller, "Preface: Educating the Whole Person" and "Holistic Education: A Brief History," in *International Handbook of Holistic Education,* xxiii-xxv, 5-16.

[34] Sam Crowell and David Reid-Marr, *Emergent Teaching: A Path to Creativity, Significance, and Transformation* (New York: Rowman Littlefield Education, 2013), 112.

[35] Brown, *Debating Yoga and Mindfulness In Public Schools*, 161-187

[36] Tim Ryan, *A Mindful Nation* (New York: Hay House, Inc., 2012).

[37] Brown, *Debating Yoga and Mindfulness in Public Schools*, 188-208.

[38] "From a Nation at Risk to a Nation at Hope: Recommendations from the National Commission on Social, Emotional, & Academic Development" (The Aspen Institute, 2018). https://wwwcasel.org.

[39] Linda Lantieri, "Preface" and "A Vision of Schools with Spirit," in Schools with Spirit, ed. Linda Lantieri (Boston: Beacon Press, 2001), xi-xvii, 7-20.

[40] Rachael Kessler, *The Soul of Education* (Alexandria, Va.: ASCD, 2000), 159. For an overview of the way the Passage-Works Institute has built on and developed Rachael Kessler's vision of what a teacher should be, see Laura Weaver & Mark Wilding, *The Dimensions of Engaged Teaching: A Practical Guide for Educators* (Bloomington, IN.: Solution Tree Press, 2013).

[41] For a further account of Tim Shriver's experience and outlook, see Lisa Miller, *The Awakened Brain: The New Science of Spirituality and Our Quest for An Inspired Life* (New York: Random House, 2021), 224-229. Regarding the possibility of court challenges in connection with efforts to promote spirituality in education, see Candy Gunther Brown, *Debating Yoga and Mindfulness in Public Schools*.

[42] www.icivics.org.

[43] Educating For American Democracy (EAD) Initiative, "Educating For American Democracy: Excellence in History and Civics for All Learners" (iCivics, March 2, 2021), 8, 10. www.educatingforamericandemocracy.org. EAD@icivics.org.

[44] Ibid., 8-22, 25-26.

[45] Ibid., 13-17.

[46] "Spirituality and the Common Good" is a statement issued

by the Common Good Collaborative (CGC), which was formed by seven leading organizations in the field of civic education in response to the coronavirus pandemic. The statement is signed by leaders from these seven organizations, which include the Bill of Rights Institute, Facing History and Ourselves, Generation Citizen, iCivics, National Constitution Center, and Mikva Challenge. Regarding its programs, CGC states: "At its core, this project is about reconnecting millions of Americans of all ages to our nation's unifying civic creeds of liberty, equality, and self-government." The project emphasizes the American citizen's "civic duty to promote the common good."

[47] Lisa Miller, *The Spiritual Child* (New York: St. Martin's Press, 2015).

[48] Ibid., 2-3, 9, 15, 28.

Chapter 5 – Science, Religion, and Natural Spirituality

[49] John Herman Randall, Jr., *Making of the Modern Mind*, 253-255, 273-279, 282-306.

[50] William James, *The Varieties of Religious Experience* (New York: University Books, 1963), 28-34, 379, 430-437, 447.

[51] Ibid., 45-52, 247, 505, 536-537.

[52] Ibid., See Lectures VI, VII, VIII.

[53] Ibid., 41, 51-52, 149-157, 184-187, 424, 486, 505.

[54] William James as quoted in *Ralph Barton Perry, The Thought and Character of William James* (Westport, Conn.: Greenwood Press, Publishers, 1974), vol. II, 328.

[55] James, *Varieties*, 73, 388; Perry, Thought and Character of William James, II, 327.

[56] James, *Varieties*, 427, 484, 525.

[57] Ibid., 334-338, 455, 594.

[58] Ewert Cousins, "Preface to the Series," in *World Spirituality: An Encyclopedic History of the Religious Quest*, ed. Ewert Cousins (Crossroad Publishing Company, 1978-1996). It is noteworthy that beginning in 1978, the Paulist Press began publishing "The Classics of Western Spirituality: A Library of the Great Spiritual

Masters." As of 2021 a total of 130 volumes have been published in the series, which includes spiritual writings from the Catholic, Protestant, Eastern Orthodox, Jewish, Islamic, and Native American traditions.

[59] *Spirituality and the Secular Quest,* ed. Peter H. Van Ness (New York: Crossroad Publishing Company, 1996), 1-16. This collection of essays is vol. 22 in the World Spirituality series.

[60] (Oxford, Oxford University Press, 2012).

[61] See Plato's dialogues "Apology," "Crito," "Symposium," and "The Republic," in *The Works of Plato,* ed. Irwin Edman (New York: The Modern Library, 1956).

[62] Leo Tolstoy, *The Death of Ivan Ilych and Other Stories* (New York: New American Library, 1960), 95-156. Leo Tolstoy, *A Confession, The Gospel in Brief, and What I Believe,* Aylmer Maude, trans. (London: Oxford University Press, 1971).

Chapter 6 – To Have and To Be

[63] Walter Kaufman, "I and You: A Prologue," in Martin Buber, *I and Thou,* trans. Walter Kaufman (New York: Charles Scribner's Sons, 1970), 32, 38. On the life of Martin Buber, see Paul Mendes-Flohr, *Martin Buber: A Life of Faith and Dissent* (New Haven: Yale University Press, 2019).

[64] Regarding the translation of the German pronoun *Du* as Thou, Paul Mendes-Flohr explains that "the familiar second person German pronoun, *Du,* is conventionally restricted to addressing close friends, relatives, and children – yet one also addresses God as Du, which since the King James Bible translation had been represented as Thou." Most Buber scholars have translated Du as Thou and *Ich-Du* as I-Thou. However, in Walter Kaufman's popular English translation, with the exception of the book title, Du is rendered as You. Mendes-Flohr, *Martin Buber,* 140-143. Kaufman, "I and You: A Prologue," 14-15.

[65] Martin Buber, *I and Thou,* 53-89. See also Martin Buber, *Hasidism and Modern Man,* trans. Maurice Friedman (New York: Harper Torchbooks, 1958), 21-43, 126-176.

[66] Viktor E. Frankl, *Man's Search for Meaning: An Introduction to Logotherapy,* trans. Ilse Lasch (Boston: Beacon Press, 1959), 77, 110-117.

[67] Erich Fromm, *To Have or To Be?* (New York: Harper & Row Publishers, 1976), xxii, 10, 65.

[68] Ibid., 8.

[69] Ibid., 24.

[70] Ibid., 65, 88.

[71] Ibid., 100, 105.

[72] Ibid., 104-105.

[73] Ibid., 106, 202.

[74] His Holiness The Dalai Lama, *Beyond Religion* (New York: Mariner Books, 2012).

[75] Ibid., ix-xv, 94-95.

[76] Ibid., xiv-xv, 12-13, 18.

[77] Ibid., xi, 5, 17, 19, 48, 1.

[78] Ibid., 50.

[79] Ibid., 52.

[80] The Dalai Lama, *A Policy of Kindness: An Anthology of Writings By and About the Dalai Lama*, ed. Sidney Piburn (New York: Snow Lion Publications, 1990), 88-89.

[81] The Dalai Lama, *Beyond Religion*, 56, 94-95, 187.

[82] Haidt, *The Righteous Mind*, xviii.

[83] Ibid., xviii, xxii, 150, 228-229, 255.

[84] Ibid., xx, 3-31, 52-61, 74-79, 134-135.

[85] Ibid., xix, xxii, 152-153, 219-258.

[86] Ibid., 52-53, 111-149, 197-216.

[87] Ibid., 214-216, 319-366.

[88] Ibid., 118-130.

[89] Ibid. xxii, 173-174, 193, 225, 256-270, 283-284.

[90] Ibid., 259, 275-279, 281-281.

[91] Jonathon Haidt, "How Social Media Made American Stupid," *The Atlantic* (May 2022). https://www.theatlantic.com/magazine/archive/2022/05 social -media-democracy-trust-babel/629369.

Chapter 7 – Awakened Awareness and America's Schools

[92] Lisa Miller, *The Awakened Brain*, 5, 13-14, 17-19.

[93] Ibid., 3, 6, 79, 145.

[94] Ibid., 44, 53, 216, 221.

[95] Ibid., 143, 209, 220-221.

[96] Ibid., 7, 148-150, 162.

[97] Ibid., 7, 148-150, 162.

[98] Ibid., 51 60.

[99] Ibid., 61-62, 141.

[100] Ibid., 222-223.

[101] Ibid., 121, 163-170.

[102] Ibid., 9-10, 224, 235, 237. For information on the Awakened Schools Institute and the 11 Drivers of a spiritually supportive school culture, see the CSE website: www.spiritualityineducation.org.

Chapter 8 – Conclusion: A Transformative Movement

[103] Bob Chapman and Raj Sisodia, *Everybody Matters* (Penguin Random House UK, 2015).

Bibliography

Baldwin, James. *The Fire Next Time.* New York: Vintage International, 1963.

Bellah, Robert N. et al. *Habits of the Heart: Individualism and Commitment in American Life.* Berkeley: University of California Press, 1985.

Berry, Thomas. *Evening Thoughts: Reflecting on Earth as a Sacred Community.* Edited by Mary Evelyn Tucker. San Francisco: Sierra Club Books, 2006.

—. *The Sacred Universe: Earth, Spirituality, and Religion in The Twentieth* Century. Edited by Mary Evelyn Tucker. New York: Columbia University Press, 2009.

Brown, Candy Gunther. *Debating Yoga and Mindfulness in Public Schools: Reforming Secular Education or Reestablishing Religion?* Chapel Hill: University of North Carolina 2019.

Buber, Martin. *I and Thou.* Translated by Walter Kaufman. New York: Charles Scribner's Sons, 1970.

—. *Hasidism and Modern Man.* Translated by Maurice Friedman. New York: Harper Torchbooks, 1958.

Chapman, Bob and Raj Sisodia. *Everybody Matters: The Extraordinary Power of Caring for Your People Like Family.* Penguin Random House UK, 2015.

Chancey, Mark A. "The Bible and American Public Schools." *The Oxford Handbook of Religion and American Education,* edited by Michael D. Waggoner and Nathan C. Walker. Oxford, Oxford University Press, 2018.

Cohen, Warren Lee and David Bresnihan. "Waldorf Education: Freeing the Human Being." In *International Handbook of Holistic Education*, edited by John P. Miller et al. New York: Routledge, 2019.

Commission on the Practice of Democratic Citizenship. *Our Common Purpose: Reinventing American Democracy For the 21st Century. Cambridge,* Mass.: American Academy of Arts & Sciences, 2020.

Cousins, Ewert, ed. *World Spirituality: An Encyclopedic History of the Religious Quest.* 25 vols. New York: Crossroad Publishing Company, 1978-1996.

Cremin, Lawrence A. *American Education: The National Experience, 1783-1876.* New York: Harper & Row, Publishers, 1980.

—. *The Transformation of the School: Progressivism in American Education, 1876-1957.* New York: Alfred Knopf, 1961.

Crowell, Sam and David Reid-Marr. *Emergent Teaching: A Path to Creativity, Significance, and Transformation.* New York: Rowman Littlefield Education, 2013.

Dewey, John. *The Ethics of Democracy.* In *John Dewey: The Early Works, 1882-1898,* edited by Jo Ann Boydston, 1: 227-249. Carbondale, Ill.: Southern Illinois University Press, 1969.

—. "My Pedagogic Creed." In *Early Works* 5: 84-95.

—. *The School and Society.* In *John Dewey: The Middle Works, 1899-1924,* edited by Jo Ann Boydston, 1: 1-109.

—. *Democracy and Education. Middle Works* 9.

—. *A Common Faith.* In *John Dewey: The Later Works, 1925-1953,* edited by Jo Ann Boydston, 9: 1-58.

—. *Liberalism and Social Action.* In *Later Works* 11: 1-65.

—. *Experience and Education.* In *Later Works* 13: 1-62.

—. *Freedom and Culture.* In *Later Works* 13: 63-188.

—. "Creative Democracy – The Task Before Us." In *Later Works* 14: 224-230.

Dorer, Michael, Tim Seldin, Robin Howe, and Jennie Caskey. "Holism in Montessori." In *International Handbook of Holistic Education*, edited by John P. Miller et al. New York: Routledge, 2019.

Earth Charter. http://www.earthcharter.org.

Educating for American Democracy (EAD) Initiative. "Educating for American Democracy: Excellence in History and Civics for All Learners." iCivics,2021. EAD@icivics.org. www.educatingforamericandemocracy.org.

Frankl, Viktor E. *Man's Search for Meaning: An Introduction to Logotherapy.* Translated by Ilse Lasch. Boston: Beacon Press, 1959.

From a Nation at Risk to a Nation at Hope: Recommendations from the National Commission on Social, Emotional, & Academic Development. Aspen Institute, 2018 https://wwwcasel.org.

Fromm, Erich H. *Escape From Freedom.* New York: Henry Holt and Company, 1965.

—. *The Art of Loving*, edited by Ruth Nanda Anshen. Harper & Brothers Publishers, 1956.

—. *To Have or To Be?*, edited by Ruth Nanda Anshen. New York: Harper & Row, Publishers, 1976

Gipe, Robert. "Appalachia Is More Diverse Than You Think." New York Times OpEd, March 16, 2019.

Gorman, Amanda. *The Hill We Climb: An Inaugural Poem for the Country.* New York: Viking, 2021.

Gorski, Philip. *American Covenant: A History of Civil Religion from the Puritans to the Present.* Princeton: Princeton University Press, 2017.

Haidt, Jonathon. *The Righteous Mind: Why Good People Are Divided by Politics and Religion.* New York: Vintage Books, 2012.

—. "How Social Media Made America Stupid." *The Atlantic* (May 2022). https://www.theatlantic.com/magazine/archive/2022/05/social-media-democracy-trust-babel/629369/

Hanh, Thich Nhat. *Peace Is Every Step: The Path of Mindfulness in Everyday Life*, edited by Arnold Kotler. New York: Bantam Books, 1991.

His Holiness The Dalai Lama. *A Policy of Kindness: An Anthology of Writings By and About The Dalai Lama*, edited by Sidney Piburn. Ithaca, N.Y.: Snow Lion Publications, 1990.

—. *Beyond Religion: Ethics for a Whole World.* New York: Mariner Books, 2012.

Hughes, Langston. *The Collected Poems of Langston Hughes.*
Edited by Arnold Rampersad. New York: Alfred Knopf,
1994.

James, William. *The Varieties of Religious Experience: A Study in
Human Nature.* New York: University Books, 1963.

Kessler, Rachael. *The Soul of Education: Helping Students Find
Connection, Compassion, and Character at School.*
Alexandria, Va.: ASCD, 2000.

Lantieri, Linda, ed. *Schools with Spirit: Nurturing the Inner Lives
of Children and Teachers.* Boston: Beacon Press, 2001.

Lappé, Frances Moore, and Paul Martin DuBois. *The Quickening
of America: Rebuilding Our Nation, Remaking Our Lives.*
San Francisco: Jossey-Bass, Inc. Publishers, 1994.

Lepore, Jill. *These Truths: A History of the United States.* New York:
W. W. Norton & Company, 2018.

Mendes-Flohr, Paul. *Martin Buber: A Life of Faith and Dissent.*
New Haven: Yale University Press, 2019.

Miller, John P. *Love and Compassion: Exploring Their Role in
Education.* Toronto: University of Toronto Press, 2018.

—. *Whole Child Education.* Toronto: University of Toronto Press,
2010.

Miller, John P. and Kelli Nigh, Marni J. Binder, Bruce Novak,
and Sam Crowell, eds. *International Handbook of Holistic
Education.* New York: Routledge, 2019.

Miller, Lisa. *The Spiritual Child: The New Science on Parenting for Health and Life Long Thriving.* New York: St. Martin's Press, 2015.

—. *The Awakened Brain: The New Science of Spirituality and Our Quest for An Inspired Life.* New York: Random House, 2021.

—. ed. T*he Oxford Handbook of Psychology and Spirituality.* Oxford: Oxford University Press, 2012. 2nd Edition forthcoming.

Palmer, Parker J. *Healing the Heart of Democracy: The Courage to Create a Politics Worthy of the Human Spirit.* San Francisco: Josey-Bass, 2011.

Perry, Ralph Barton. *The Thought and Character of William James.* Westport, Conn.: Greenwood Press, Publishers, 1974.

Plato. *The Works of Plato.* Edited by Irwin Edman. Translated by Benjamin Jowett. New York: The Modern Library, 1956.

Prothero, Stephen. *Religious Literacy: What Every American Needs to Know – and Doesn't.* New York: HarperCollins Publisher, 2008.

Putnam, Robert D. and Shaylyn Romney Garrett. *The Upswing: How America Came Together a Century Ago and How We Can Do It Again.* New York: Simon & Schuster, 2020.

Randall, John Herman, Jr. *The Making of the Modern Mind.* Houghton Mifflin Company, 1940.

Rockefeller, Steven C. *John Dewey: Religious Faith and Democratic Humanism.* New York: Columbia University Press, 1991.

—. "Crafting Principles for the Earth Charter." In *A Voice for Earth: American Writers Respond to the Earth Charter*, edited by Peter Blaze Corcoran and James Wohlpart. Athens, Georgia: University of Georgia Press, 2008.

—. *Democratic Equality, Economic Inequality, and the Earth Charter*. San Jose, Costa Rica: Earth Charter International, 2015.

—. "Ecological and Social Responsibility: The Making of the Earth Charter." In *Responsibility*, edited by Barbara Darling-Smith. Lanham, MD: Rowman & Littlefield Publishers, Inc., 2007.

—. "Faith and Community in an Ecological Age." In *Spirit and Nature: Why the Environment Is a Religious Issue*, edited by Steven C. Rockefeller and John Elder. Boston: Beacon Press, 1992.

—. "Renewing the American Democratic Faith." In *Democracy Unchained: How to Rebuild Government for the People*, edited by David W. Orr et al. New York: The New Press, 2020.

Ryan, Tim. *A Mindful Nation: How a Simple Practice Can Help Us Reduce Stress, Improve Performance, and Recapture the American Spirit*. New York: Hay House, Inc., 2012.

Sandel, Michael J. *Democracy's Discontent: America in Search of a Public Philosophy*. Belknap Press of Harvard University Press, 1996.

Schlesinger, Arthur M., Jr. *The Disuniting of America*. New York: W.W. Norton & Company, 1992.

Speth, James Gustave. *The Bridge at the Edge of the World: Capitalism, the Environment, and Crossing From Crisis to Sustainability.* New Haven and London: Yale University Press, 2008.

Swimme, Brian and Thomas Berry. *The Universe Story: From The Primordial Flaring Forth to the Ecozoic Era – A Celebration of the Unfolding of the Cosmos.* Harper San Francisco, 1992.

Swimme, Brian and Mary Evelyn Tucker. *Journey of the Universe.* New Haven: Yale University Press, 2011. https//wwwjourneyoftheuniverse.org.

Taylor, A. E. *Plato: The Man and His Work.* New York: The World Publishing Company, 1963.

Tolstoy, Leo. *The Death of Ivan Ilych and Other Stories.* New York: New American Library, 1960.

—. A Confession, *The Gospel in Brief, and What I Believe,* translated by Aylmer Maude. London: Oxford University Press, 1971.

Tucker, Mary Evelyn, John Grim, and Andrew Angyal. *Thomas Berry: A Biography.* New York: Columbia University Press, 2019.

Van Ness, Peter H., ed. *Spirituality and the Secular Quest.* In *World Spirituality: An Encyclopedic History of the Religious Quest*, edited by Ewert Cousins, vol. 22. New York: Crossroad Publishing Company, 1996.

Vilela, Mirian and Alicia Jimenez, eds. *Earth Charter, Education and the Sustainable Development Goal 4.7: Research, Experiences and Reflections.* San Jose, Costa Rica: University for Peace Press, 2020.

Weaver, Laura and Mark Wilding. *The Dimensions of Engaged Teaching: A Practical Guide for Educators.* Bloomington, IN.: Solution Tree Press, 2013.

Westbrook, Robert B. *John Dewey and American Democracy.* Ithaca, N.Y.: Cornell University Press, 1991.

Whitman, Walt. *Democratic Vistas.* Edited by Ed Folsom. Iowa City IA: University of Iowa Press, 2010.

Wood, Gordon S. *Power and Liberty: Constitutionalism in the American Revolution.* Oxford University Press, 2021.

Acknowledgments

The writing of *Spiritual Democracy and Our Schools* has been inspired by my involvement over the last six years with the Collaborative for Spirituality in Education (CSE), a not-for-profit organization that is based at Teachers College, Columbia University. It was through many in-depth conversations with Professor Lisa Miller, a principal leader in the field of spirituality in education, that a friend and former business leader, Frank Peabody and I were introduced to this field of innovative research and promising educational reform. From these conversations emerged the idea of creating CSE to support Professor Miller's research and her vision for promoting spirituality in education in K–12 schools nationwide. Working together with Lisa Miller, who serves as the founding president of CSE, and Frank Peabody, with whom I co-chair the CSE board of trustees, has been an especially rewarding experience.

In the course of seeking to understand the challenges CSE faces and to support its mission, I encountered some complex questions regarding spirituality and education. I also began to see some important connections with my own earlier research in the fields of religion, spirituality, ethics, democracy, and American philosophy. In an address in 2019 at a CSE conference, I outlined some of my initial thinking regarding the historical background and the critical significance of the contemporary movement in support of spirituality in education. Responding to an invitation from Lisa Miller to turn that address into an essay for publication, as I got more deeply into the subject, the essay kept expanding and evolved into the book, *Spiritual Democracy and Our Schools*.

The writing of this book would not have been possible without the encouragement, support, and assistance of a number of colleagues. I am deeply grateful to Lisa Miller and Frank Peabody for their support of this project and for their comments and recommendations on drafts of the book as it took form. Amy Chapman, the CSE Director, reviewed drafts, and I very much appreciate her support and comments. Two longtime friends and colleagues, Professor Rueben Rainey and Professor Mary Evelyn Tucker, kindly agreed to read a draft as it was nearing completion, and I want to extend to them my deep thanks for their thoughtful reflections and recommendations.

I have learned much from the dialogue among the members of the CSE board of trustees and thank them for sharing their insights and experience. There has been a strong partnership between CSE and the Fetzer Institute since the founding of CSE, and Fetzer's philanthropic mission and leadership in support of spirituality, a culture of love, renewal of democracy, and education of the whole child has been a source of inspiration. Bob Boisture, president of the Fetzer Institute, serves as a member of the CSE board of trustees, and I extend my appreciation and gratitude to him and to his Fetzer colleagues, Jonathan Lever and Xiaoan Li.

Josephine Reyes has provided assistance with research and with the preparation of electronic drafts of the text as it evolved. She has also helped to manage related correspondence. I extend many, many thanks to her. I thank Leslie George for her contributions to the project as a proofreader, including the thoughtful questions she raised about writing style. Frances Beebe has coordinated the process of putting the manuscript in final form, designed the book, and made all arrangements for the printing and initial distribution of the book. I appreciate very much the careful planning and assistance she has provided and to her, I extend special thanks.

When I think about what has made the writing of this book possible, nothing has been more important than the love and support of my wife, Barbara. She is an American historian, and especially since social contacts have been greatly restricted by the pandemic, our ongoing dialogue regarding religion, spirituality,

American history, current events, and the art of writing has been a special gift as the writing of this book progressed.

SCR

About the Author

Steven C. Rockefeller is professor emeritus of religion at Middlebury College, where he also served as dean of the College. He received his master of divinity degree from Union Theological Seminary in New York City and his Ph.D. in the philosophy of religion from Columbia University. He is the author of *John Dewey: Religious Faith and Democratic Humanism* (Columbia, 1991) and the co-editor of two books of essays, *The Christ and the Bodhisattva* (SUNY, 1987) and *Spirit and Nature: Why the Environment is a Religious Issue* (Beacon, 1992). His essays appear in many books and journals. One major focus of interest in his writing is the interrelation of spirituality, democracy, and ecology. Bill Moyers conducts an interview with Professor Rockefeller in Moyer's World of Ideas television series.

Professor Rockefeller was centrally involved in the creation of the Earth Charter, an international declaration of global interdependence with fundamental principles for building a just, sustainable, and peaceful world. Active in the field of philanthropy, for three decades, he served as a trustee of the Rockefeller Brothers Fund (RBF) and chaired the Fund's board from 1998 to 2006. Among the other boards and commissions on which he has served are the National Commission on the Environment, the National Audubon Society, and the Colonial Williamsburg Foundation. He was the founding president of the Wendell Gilley Museum in Southwest Harbor, Maine, and of the Otter Creek Child Care Center in Middlebury, Vermont. He led the collaborative effort to create the Charlotte Park and Wildlife Refuge in Vermont, which overlooks Lake Champlain and the Adirondack Mountains. Since 2017, he has served as co-chair of the board of trustees for the Collaborative for Spirituality in Education.

Professor Rockefeller is married to the American historian, Barbara Bellows Rockefeller. He has four children, nine grandchildren, and two great-grandchildren.

Index